"I've always had a love for life, enthusiasm, vision, and the desire to create something different, even when I was a boy in Santiago de Cuba and didn't know too much about the world beyond my own. No dream was ever too unobtainable or absurd. If I wanted to do something, I began by believing I could. I arrived in the United States with the clothes on my back and nothing but a suitcase full of dreams and a heart filled with hope and optimism. That, it seems, was enough."

—from *The Rhythm of Success*

Praise for
The Rhythm of Success

"*The Rhythm of Success* is both motivational and inspirational . . . and it reads very conversationally. While Estefan has indeed produced his own American dream, you don't for a minute feel as if he has taken it for granted. Rather, you get the sense that he has appreciated every moment of it—so much so that he wants to share his life experiences and philosophies so that others might benefit from them and make their own dreams come true."

—*Hartford Books Examiner*

"A perfect present for music fans."
—nochelatina.com

THE RHYTHM OF SUCCESS

How an Immigrant Produced
His Own American Dream

EMILIO ESTEFAN

A CELEBRA BOOK

Celebra
Published by New American Library,
a division of Penguin Group (USA) Inc.,
375 Hudson Street, New York, New York 10014, USA
Penguin Group (Canada), 90 Eglinton Avenue East, Suite 700, Toronto,
Ontario M4P 2Y3, Canada (a division of Pearson Penguin Canada Inc.)
Penguin Books Ltd., 80 Strand, London WC2R 0RL, England
Penguin Ireland, 25 St. Stephen's Green, Dublin 2,
Ireland (a division of Penguin Books Ltd.)
Penguin Group (Australia), 250 Camberwell Road, Camberwell,
Victoria 3124, Australia (a division of Pearson Australia Group Pty. Ltd.)
Penguin Books India Pvt. Ltd., 11 Community Centre,
Panchsheel Park, New Delhi - 110 017, India
Penguin Group (NZ), 67 Apollo Drive, Rosedale, North Shore 0632,
New Zealand (a division of Pearson New Zealand Ltd.)
Penguin Books (South Africa) (Pty.) Ltd., 24 Sturdee Avenue,
Rosebank, Johannesburg 2196, South Africa

Penguin Books Ltd., Registered Offices:
80 Strand, London WC2R 0RL, England

Published by Celebra, an imprint of New American Library, a division of Penguin Group (USA) Inc.
Previously published in a Celebra hardcover edition.

First Celebra Trade Paperback Printing, January 2011
10 9 8 7 6 5 4 3 2 1

Celebra Trade Paperback ISBN: 978-0-451-23077-5

The Library of Congress has cataloged the hardcover edition of this title as follows:

Estefan, Emilio.
The rhythm of success: how an immigrant produced his own American dream/Emilio Estefan.
p. cm.
ISBN 978-0-451-22642-6
1. Success—United States 2. Immigrants—United States 3. Hispanic Americans.
4. United States—Emigration and immigration—Economic aspects. I. Title.
BF637.S8.E88 2010
650.1—dc22 2009031730

Set in Simoncini Garamond
Designed by Ginger Legato

Printed in the United States of America

*To any young kid with the dream of becoming
the first Hispanic President of the United States*

ACKNOWLEDGMENTS

The following people have played an important part in my life and I want to thank them for their love and support:

Carmen and Emilio Estefan—for without them, this story would not be possible.
Gloria, Nayib and Emily Estefan
Jose "Papo," Patricia, and Jennifer Estefan
Gloria Fajardo
Lili, Lorenzo, Lorenzito, Lina (Angelina) Luaces
Juan "Michy" Estefan
Rebecca Fajardo
Frank Amadeo
Ricardo Dopico
Cathleen Farrell
Quincy Jones
Phil Ramone
Tommy Mottola
Janet de Armas
Jose Maldonado
Raymond Garcia
The entire staff at Estefan Enterprises, Inc.
The staff at Crescent Moon Studios

CONTENTS

FOREWORD

E milio Estefan is the Ambassador of Latin music in the U.S. He has a sense of pride and heritage so deep that it emanates through everything he touches. All of his greatest accomplishments were made possible because of one reason—he does what he loves.

I can relate to Emilio in so many ways. When I was growing up, there were no black idols doing what I would ultimately do. I had to make my own dream. Man, when I was a kid, all I wanted to be was a gangster. I got into all types of serious trouble, but I distinctly recall the day my life changed. I was eleven years old when I broke into a local recreation center and snuck into an administration room, where in a dark corner I saw a piano. I almost walked out and closed the door shut. But thank God a voice came to me and said, "Idiot, get back in that room." I opened that door, sat at the piano, slowly put my fingers over the keys and started to play. Every bone in my body told me music would be in my life, heart and soul forever. I played instruments in school before then, but I didn't really know how to make music. I just always loved it. But, at that moment, as much as I needed food and water to survive, I knew I would need music to live. I thank God that at eleven years old that piano saved my life.

When Emilio was growing up in the U.S., there were no Latin music moguls for him to emulate. He had to make his own dream, too. Emilio found his love for music at an early age with his accordion. He knew music ran deep in his veins and it would be with him as long as he lived. Like me, when he was eleven years old, his life changed. He was forced to leave Cuba with the responsibility of bringing his family to America. While Castro stripped him of his life as he knew it, he couldn't take away his passion for his culture, his determination to succeed and his love for music. Emilio came to America and single-handedly made Latin music a pop-cultural craze with the Miami Sound Machine, opened doors for so many new artists, like Ricky Martin and Shakira, and helped preserve the incredible influence of Cuban music with legends, like Israel Cachao Lopez and Celia Cruz.

I understand Emilio so well because I love Cuban music so much. It's a lot like jazz. It has classic, African, rumba and so many other influences. At the age of nineteen, I was blessed to go to Cuba, while Batista was president, and really grasped the origins of these amazingly technical and soulful sounds. The people, colors, and music of that island will stay with me always. By the time I was twenty-two, I was already mixing with Dizzy Gillespie, and some of the greatest Cuban precisionists of all time, like the ultimate conga showman Carlos "Patato" Valdez, who was in my band; the masterful Candido Camero; and the pioneering Chano Pozo. In the early 1950s, I was going with Brando to the Palladium every Sunday to see Latin music giants like Chico O'Farrill, Tito Puente, Johnny Pacheco, Machito, Mario Bauzá and countless other legendary performers. That music burned through the dance floor like wild fire, man. That's the energy Emilio has within him.

I've had the honor of arranging and recording with the greatest names in music, like Ella Fitzgerald, Louis Armstrong, Aretha Franklin, Lionel Hampton, Sarah Vaughan, Ray Charles, Count Basie, Duke Ellington, Billie Holiday, and Miles Davis, just to name a few. I spotted a new generation of talent, like the late and incomparable Michael Jackson, Oprah, and Will Smith. Throughout the years, I've met and worked with so many thousands of amazing people all over the world. And, I'm telling you, there is just a feeling you get when you meet someone that is so real. Emilio is as real as it gets. His extraordinary wife and my baby sister, Gloria, his son and my homeboy, Nayib and his daughter and my precious goddaughter, Emily, are all truly my family—my blood. They will always have my eternal love.

I've lived my entire life by the fundamental principle that "not one drop of myself depends on your acceptance of me." Because Emilio and I had to create our own paths, we had to believe in our dreams no matter what anybody said. We overcame every hurdle in order to make our music heard. The music we were playing had nothing to do with money or fame. Believe me, you didn't play bebop or Cuban music to get rich. We only did what we loved. There was a rhythm to our success. We just listened to it and followed it. And, if there is anyone that could possibly inspire you to listen to the rhythm of your own success and follow it, it's my brother, Emilio Estefan.

In the following pages, you will learn a lot about an extraordinary man but, more important, about your own extraordinary potential.

—Quincy Jones

THE RHYTHM
OF SUCCESS

Emilio Estefan at age six swimming in Cuba.

Introduction

My childhood ended when I was eleven. I know the exact instant that it happened. Standing unseen at a door in our house, I overheard my parents talking about the situation that lay ahead for our country and ultimately our family. If you understand that this episode took place in the mid-1960s and the country we lived in was Cuba, you'll know I heard nothing encouraging, nothing that would make me optimistic for the years ahead. My parents spoke with such worry in their voices that it frightened me. Many people close to us had already left Cuba, including children I had gone to school with, and others were quietly making plans. There was so much uncertainty.

Although at first what I heard scared me, I was very quickly filled with an extraordinary sense of purpose. In the course of those few moments I was a little boy no longer. Instantly I became a man.

As my parents talked about Castro's revolution and the direction it was taking, I knew what I'd have to do. I was going to have to take on a great responsibility and leave my country if my family was going to have any future together. As parents do they worried about their children. By this time my older brother, who was already of military age, was at the university studying engineering and there was no way the government would allow him to leave Cuba. But I was several years away from the age when I might be required for military service, and young enough

3

that I could potentially leave. That day I had no real plan, just the realization that leaving Cuba was my only way to live in a free world. I knew I was my family's only hope.

What does the concept of freedom mean to an eleven-year-old boy? I couldn't have told you anything about constitutional government or life, liberty, and the pursuit of happiness. I just knew that freedom was a place where soldiers didn't come to your home and herd people around with machine guns—something that had just happened to our family. I knew that freedom was a place where the government couldn't simply take money from you just because they wanted to—it was U.S. dollars the soldiers were looking for in our house. At that moment, standing outside my parents' room, I probably wouldn't have been able to give freedom a name, but I did know it existed in the United States of America, and I knew that my family's future depended on me to find it.

The long-term goal was to reunite our family in the United States. I wasn't able to leave on my own, and my mother wasn't willing to leave her parents. That left me and my dad. I knew that I had to convince my mother to let us leave, to make her see that we'd have to separate in order to have a future where we could all live together in freedom. In the wake of the Bay of Pigs invasion and the terrible state of U.S.-Cuban relations, we had to find a third country to live in the meantime, and we settled on Spain.

Cuba is only ninety miles from Florida. So close and yet so far. I used to look at the water that kissed the sand of our beautiful Cuban beaches and imagine that it had touched the United States—the two countries felt so close! I used to also look into the sky and think how people all over the world looked at the same sky. Except they looked at it through eyes of freedom.

This was a terrifying time for me. The decision was my responsibility. My father wasn't a man who made plans; my mother didn't want us to leave. She felt terribly conflicted, not wanting to leave her father but she knew at heart it was the right thing for my father and me to do. When it finally was time for us to get on the plane and fly out of Havana my heart was broken.

As I headed out into the unknown my greatest fear was that I'd never see my mother again. When I hugged my mother and brother good-bye, I didn't know if I would ever see them again. I thought this might be the last hug I would ever give them. As I hugged my grandfather and said good-bye, I felt as if I were burying someone alive. When I looked into my grandfather's eyes, I knew I would never see him again.

I was right.

As the plane taxied down the runway my hand was pressed to the glass of the window and I was crushed by sadness. There was no turning back. It was odd seeing other people on the plane, some happy and smiling with their families as they were returning to Spain. But for me, I didn't know if I would ever return home. I didn't know what the future held for me.

My father and I had very tough times in Spain. We were close to being homeless, and we ate from a soup kitchen most days. We weren't allowed to work so it was impossible to support ourselves. It was the most difficult year and a half of my life. But I knew in the end, the struggle would be worth it. Eighteen months later I traveled on my own from Spain to Miami with the single hope of reuniting my family. That hope never wavered, but my journey was far from complete. All through this period and beyond I was driven by the same energy and persistence that I as an eleven-year-old possessed when I overheard my parents talking about the darkness that lay ahead for Cuba.

As difficult as that period was, I remain grateful to Spain for giving us our first refuge. And I value that experience, as painful as it often was, because it helped me form the values that have guided me through my life.

Occasionally certain things will happen that remind me how far I've come and how fortunate I've been in my life. A couple of years ago Gloria and I were on vacation, along with our daughter, Emily, and we flew from the beautiful city of Prague in the Czech Republic to Madrid. Emily was about the same age I was when I had arrived, about forty years earlier with my father. All of a sudden I felt overwhelmed by a sense of déjà vu and then mixed emotions. I felt sadness but I also had an incredible feeling of joy and pride to arrive with my own family, real-izing how different life was from the time that I first walked that corri-dor with my father. I had come full circle in life. It made me realize more than ever that the decision I made forty years earlier to leave Cuba was the right one. Because of that decision my family was able to live in freedom.

At heart, I'm the same guy now that I was then: determined, full of life and energy, and ready to take on any challenge that life brings my way. Though the younger me was a hopeful immigrant on a search for freedom, the older me is now living the American dream, with an amaz-ing wife of thirty years and my two beautiful children.

In this book, I hope you find my guiding philosophy, which I believe has helped me to achieve professional success and tremendous personal happiness. My values are at the core of all my actions and my whole life I have known that the best guarantee for a positive outcome is a positive attitude at the outset. I have long known how to turn negatives into posi-tives and how to turn things around. I am also a great believer in plan-ning for the long term, as is illustrated by these few stories I've just shared.

Most of all, I have always followed my heart and my intuition—I've done what I love and I believe in myself and in my ideas and dreams.

Together Gloria and I have worked very hard to create a hugely suc-cessful enterprise that includes music publishing, restaurants, hotels, music, and film and television production. But I didn't come to this country with the goal of fame and fortune.

I came for freedom. I've always remembered my heritage, and where I came from is a vital part of who I am. I haven't imitated; I have created. As a percussionist it's fair to say I've worked to my own beat—that's the rhythm of my success.

The first beats of that rhythm came when I was young, when I went from being a boy to becoming a man in the course of being a two-time immigrant. When you see me looking happy and confident and smiling in a photo, think of that young kid leaving his mom behind, terrified he'd never see her again. Because without one, the other doesn't exist.

CHAPTER ONE

Take Responsibility

I 'm an entrepreneur, and all entrepreneurs are alike in certain ways. I can think of four: We're risk takers, we're big thinkers, we're creative, and we're resourceful. Perhaps there's another: We can't sit still; we're a little bit impatient. But I'm going to put these ideas to one side for a minute (be patient!) and talk about one thing I think we don't all share.

What not all entrepreneurs have is a sense of responsibility, whether it's for themselves, the project at hand, or the people who work for them. One of my most deeply held beliefs is that responsibility is a vital feature in the makeup of an entrepreneur. And it's not just important for people who want to get ahead in business. Anyone who wants to achieve anything at all has to stand up, make decisions, and be accountable for them.

When we're young we're responsible for only ourselves. Childhood should be carefree and full of joy. As we grow up, more is added to our plates until they're full to bursting. As part of a family you share at least some responsibility for the well-being of everyone. For a kid that may just mean doing chores and helping out around the house. Then when you get a job you have duties people are relying on you to do properly. By the time you've started your own family there's serious pressure to provide for your loved ones. I've always had a very strong sense of responsibility. I think it first hit me that day I stood outside my parents' door and heard them talk about our future. I made a decision—that I'd have to be the one who would get my family out of the country—and I stood by my decision until I had finished the task. That's taking responsibility.

I was forced to make this decision and behave like a grown-up at an early age because I knew my father wasn't going to act. I loved my father to death—he taught me so much—but he wasn't a man who took responsibility like that. He was a professional gambler who lived life minute by minute. He made no plans for the future because he thought the future would take care of itself, which it does if you leave everything to chance. He was an extraordinarily generous man, and he taught me that giving was better than receiving. All his life, if my father ever had any money, he'd give it away. Even when we were down and out, if he had two dollars, he would give one away. Years later, when we were together in Miami, I'd give him things—fancy watches, expensive cars—and I'd never see them again. He'd hand them over to someone he thought needed it more than he did. My dad wanted to die with one pair of shoes and one suit to his name, and he did, despite my best efforts.

As young as I was, I was already aware of how oppressive Cuba had become. People were afraid. For a long time, there were no real business transactions because of the communist system; there was no enterprise, and legal businesses were being confiscated by the government. Before the revolution, my parents had started a business from the house, sewing underwear for a shop owned by one of my father's brothers. After the revolution, we dedicated more time to the business until it too was confiscated by the communist regime.

It seemed that more and more people's livelihoods were being taken from them. Entrepreneurs—people like my grandfather, who had always worked for himself—found it hard, if not impossible, to work for people who didn't have a clue about how to run a business. Most businesses simply began to fail. The economic disaster and getting out of the country became topics of daily conversation at my grandmother Julia's house.

The currency was changed from dollars to Cuban pesos, and those who had dollars had to convert them to pesos. It was illegal to possess U.S. dollars, or any other kind of foreign currency for that matter. When heavily armed soldiers entered our house I was shocked by the way they acted—they were so rough and aggressive. I didn't understand what was going on. They went into my parents' room. There was a painting on the wall, and behind the painting was a wall safe. When the soldiers knocked the painting off the wall, they found the safe. Of course, they automatically assumed that my parents were hoarding dollars and that my father must have been doing something illegal.

The soldier shoved all of us outside onto the patio behind the house. These guys weren't in a mood to hear arguments—not that any of us felt much like arguing. After we were outside for a few minutes, the soldiers called my father back inside. We were all very tense by this point when I heard my father arguing with one of the soldiers. My father had forgotten the combination to the safe. He hadn't used it in years, so why would he remember it? This just made things worse. The soldiers forced us all to sit down. Then they put a charge of dynamite on the safe and blew it open. All they found inside was some of my mother's old jewelry and a bunch of papers—nothing of any value, and certainly nothing illegal.

It seemed that the government's eyes were now on my father. My family had been shaken not long before by the arrest of one of my cousins, who'd gone to a foreign embassy in Havana, trying to get a visa. My aunt, who had helped my cousin, wound up spending twenty years in jail because of it. With each passing month the stakes were getting higher.

Many schoolmates and friends of mine had already left. Seeing this only strengthened my resolve to leave. Many children left Cuba on their own. Between 1960 and 1962, fourteen thousand children left Cuba under Operation Pedro Pan, the largest exodus of unaccompanied minors ever to take place in the Western Hemisphere. About half of them were reunited with relatives in the United States, while the rest were placed with American foster families who took care of them until their own parents or family members could leave. Most didn't see their families for years on end. Some families were separated forever.

I know my parents especially were terrified by that possibility. In any case, travel to the United States became impossible for three years after the Cuban Missile Crisis in October 1962. All travel between the two countries was suspended until late 1965, when both governments agreed to an airlift of Cubans who wished to relocate to the United States. But it wasn't that easy; even though the Freedom Flights lasted into the 1970s, not everyone who wanted to go could leave, like my brother, for instance.

My brother, Papo, was almost a Pedro Pan. At the start of the program, he applied for his passport and the family prepared for his departure. He was fourteen years old. The government didn't allow young men between the ages of sixteen and thirty to leave the country, because they might be needed to serve in the military, so Papo's time was running out. But when he got his passport, his last name was misspelled and so the passport wasn't valid. He turned sixteen before a new passport could be issued, so Papo couldn't go. It would be another twenty years before he could get out of Cuba.

It took a long time for my family to get used to the idea of anyone leaving the country. Perhaps it was because both sides of my family had already come to Cuba from other countries; they were more reluctant to leave too quickly. They had come looking for a better life and had built it through hard work. Both my mother's and father's parents had come to Cuba when it was still a very young country. My mother's father did not want to be an immigrant yet again.

Cuba achieved independence from Spain barely half a century prior to the revolution. I believe my grandparents and even my parents thought that this was the kind of thing a fledgling country went through—growing pains, if you will. Many people in our circle, people who stayed on those first years, believed either that Castro wasn't as bad as some thought or that he'd eventually be overthrown. Not everyone saw the revolution as an immediate threat to their way of life.

For my mother, leaving was out of the question because her own parents didn't want to go and my brother couldn't. Some members of my own family started to leave. Many of my father's relatives, his brothers and nephews, were in business for themselves, and they began to feel pressure from the communist government, believing their own businesses would be confiscated.

The first person to leave was my father's older sister, Isabel—known to everyone as Javivi (like *habibi*—Arabic for "my love") and her husband, my uncle Pepe Medina. He had a car dealership and they lived a life of relative ease. My uncle's political activities—he wrote articles and spoke out against the Castro regime—made it imperative for them to leave. They were the first to go, and they spent many years working extremely hard at menial jobs in Miami to make money to get as many of us out as possible.

All this was in the background when I overheard my parents that fateful day. I went to my mother and I told her that I had to get out so I could get all of us out. My mother could see I was absolutely determined to leave Cuba, and so the family decided that we would try to get me out, along with my father. Someone in the family realized that my father and I could probably make it to Spain. My grandparents had been born in Spain, which meant my mother was eligible for a visa, and that would allow my father and me to get a visa to travel there. Once we decided on Spain, we heard of other Cubans doing the same.

My parents began getting the paperwork to the Spanish Embassy in Havana, and my aunt Javivi began sending us money for our tickets. It was a long process, and success was never assured. During that uncertain time, my senses were more acute than I ever remembered them being before. I didn't want to sleep—I would just lie in my bed studying the ceiling. I would concentrate on trying to remember every inch of my house. And I would long after remember its smell. I was already beginning to miss my grandfather and I was still with him.

The day finally arrived—our visas were granted. It was time to go.

My brother accompanied my father and me to Havana, where the two of us would catch the flight to Spain. It was February 1967, a few weeks before my fourteenth birthday, and it would be the last time we'd all be together for another thirteen years. If I'd known that at the time, I'm not sure I'd have had the courage to get on the plane. I guess it's a good thing I didn't know.

The night before my father and I left, Papo and I walked and talked for hours. My brother was already married, with one child and one on the way. His desire to get out of Cuba was as strong as ever. I realized listening to him that I couldn't view leaving Cuba in a selfish way; I couldn't worry too much about my own feelings; I had to see the larger purpose to all of this. But leaving was so hard for me. I felt a weight on my soul.

My father and I left with nothing but the clothes on our backs. We really didn't have a lot of clothes to begin with, and Cuba was already suffering a lot of shortages. Most people who left took almost nothing with them.

I remember everything about leaving Cuba. I remember holding my father's hand as we walked up the stairs to the plane. I remember the smell of the plane. Most of all—worst of all—I remember looking out the window of the plane and seeing my mother and brother outside. When the plane began to move, I began to cry. And I cried. And I cried. And I cried all the way to Spain. It was as if my soul had left my body, I swear to God.

It was then that I realized in the most painful way possible that taking responsibility has a high cost. I didn't know the details of what might lie ahead in my life and in the lives of my family members, but in my heart of hearts I knew that this was the right thing. And I was resolute. I'd made my decision and taken on the responsibility and I stuck to it. This has been the guiding principle in all areas of my life since then.

With this decision, our family regained control over our destiny, something all of us want. But, of all the hard lessons I learned at an early age, this was the toughest and probably the most important: Taking responsibility might be painful; it might have a very high cost. Not taking responsibility could have an even higher cost.

CHAPTER TWO

Be Positive

B eing positive is a decision. You just don't wake up positive every day; you have to work at it. And a positive attitude is one of the best resources you can have. That was another important lesson I learned early on. I learned it through experience, and I learned it through example. A positive outlook is also my father's greatest legacy to me.

The plane carrying my father and me approached Madrid and landed on a runway lined with blue lights. I remember those blue lights so vividly. We arrived late in the evening; it must have been about eleven p.m. It had been a long flight, and I was exhausted both from crying and from carrying the heaviness in my heart. But the blue lights on the runway were strangely comforting, and I decided they represented a glimmer of hope.

We got off the plane and were taken to a room to fill out some forms. It was late and I was so tired and I tried not to feel disoriented. I felt miserable as I walked down the corridor in the airport. I don't know if it was the cold or the feeling of emptiness. A priest met us and took us into the city and to a shelter where we had to fill out more forms in order to receive food and to have a *pensión* assigned to us, which would become our home for months. We were grateful to have a friendly face pick us up and to have somewhere to stay.

The first thing that struck me about Madrid was the cold. I had never experienced anything like it. I was born on a tropical island and I'd never traveled anywhere outside of Cuba. My skin tingled and I shivered. It was an odd sensation. I wasn't sure it was unpleasant but it was certainly a shock. How many more was I going to experience?

I knew that Spain represented a new beginning for us, but all the time I was there I was stung by the separation from my family and the feeling that I might never see them again. I would live with two clocks, in two time zones. I often imagined what my family and friends were doing back in Cuba. "They are having lunch now," I would think. Or, "They must still be asleep," when I was already up in the morning. Many nights I lay awake thinking I'd never see my mother again. It took an enormous amount of willpower and constant pep talks to remind myself that this was a step we had to take in order to re-unite my family in freedom. The minute we landed in Spain—from the second I saw the blue lights on the runway, in fact—I knew I had to find the positive in this situation.

There's nothing's more important to me than finding the positive in everything. It explains more about me than anything. I'll find the positive angle; I'll turn the negative into a positive. Always. Every time. It's an attitude, a way of looking at the world that's been vital to my success. Take the current recession. Of course it's tough—everyone's been affected. But I see it as a time of opportunity, a time to be really creative with your assets and resources. If you see only the negative you're denying yourself a chance to succeed, even to excel.

I must have always had the seed of that attitude, but it really came to fruition when my father and I were in Spain. When we moved to our new country I was too young to get a job, and my father didn't have the right visa to allow him to work. The fact that he couldn't work didn't seem to bother him too much. Nothing ever really bothered my father. He was as happy-go-lucky as could be. He never seemed to fret or worry about things, and I don't remember him ever being sad. I wondered for years why he didn't seem down when we were in Spain, because like me he was away from his family too and I was feeling it badly.

His attitude about things, as noble as it might have been, forced me to be the responsible one for the two of us. I had to take responsibility in getting us out of Cuba and then act responsibly when we were away. He really was like a kid, and I had to become the adult: a father to my father. It happens to many of us later in life, but I was fourteen and he was in his forties, a vigorous and healthy man. I learned to be the one who planned and saved and took care of business.

But my father's refusal to be negative meant that we never gave up.

Life wasn't easy for us in Spain. We discovered that there were a lot of Cubans in the same boat as us: refugees using Spain as a staging post to get to the United States. So many people were waiting to get on with their lives, in many cases waiting to be reunited with their loved ones outside of Cuba.

We spoke the language and that should have been an advantage. But the fact was that although we were in the country legally, we weren't allowed to work. Every month, like clockwork, an envelope arrived from Miami, from my aunt Javivi, with a postal order for my father and me to pay for our *pensión* and with some left over to get by on. We stretched that money like a rubber band to make sure it lasted till the next check came. It paid for our very simple housing; we ate what we could afford and we walked when we couldn't pay for public transportation.

We spent our days waiting for visas that would allow us to travel to the United States. We also had to save money from whatever Aunt Javivi and some friends of my father in the United States would send us in order to buy tickets for our journey once we had the authorization. From Monday to Friday, my father and I would go to a church soup kitchen. They gave us soup, bread, an apple, and a bit of coffee. I remember the menu partly because it was so simple and also because it was always the same. There was never any variety, but we were grateful for the meal every time we had it.

On the weekends, the soup kitchen was closed and we had to fend for ourselves. We spent a lot of time during the days just killing time. If we ever had any extra money, my father and I would go to the cinema, but that was a rare treat. I wrote to my mother every single day, even though I knew it would take months for the letters to reach her and my brother. And she would write back to me as often as she could. *Sr. Emilio Estefan, Alcala 281, Madrid,* the envelopes read. I never knew if she and my brother had also sent letters that didn't reach me. Often letters would come cut-up, or with words blacked out by Cuban government censors.

In my letters home, I talked about Spain, detailing everything we were doing. I remember thinking as I was writing how much I wanted all my family to see what I was seeing. Even though times were often grim for us, I saw the beauty of the city and enjoyed getting to know a place that was so different from my home. I remember so clearly taking a bus in Madrid and passing by all the beautiful boutiques and stores, and looking at the shopwindows and thinking, "What a lot of clothes and shoes—so much." There was an incredible abundance of goods. And there were lights everywhere. I had come from a world that I saw as completely dark and hopeless and had arrived to one of brilliant, shiny colors. Seeing all this, I allowed myself to appreciate it even though my mother and brother couldn't. It gave me strength and made me ask God to let the rest of my family enjoy what I was experiencing too, even if it was with my nose pressed against the inside of a bus window.

There's no pretty way to put it: We were destitute. Practically penniless, we were in a foreign land, dependent on the mercy and kindness of family on the other side of the ocean. Could it have been worse? Yes, of course it could. We could have been back in the repressive society we had left in the country we loved. We loved our country but not its government, so being in Spain represented a huge step forward. Even at my young age, I felt gratitude to this country, to Spain, for giving us refuge. And I tried to keep that fact before my eyes all the time.

Of course, sometimes I would get depressed and even discouraged. How could I enjoy eating this or enjoying seeing that, I would ask myself, when my family couldn't? But our difficult times in Spain gave me even greater resolve to bring my family back together. I wanted to get ahead in this world so I could do that. My dreams were filled with thoughts of my family, of all of us together again.

The tough times in Spain prepared me for so much. The pain we lived through there, mainly because of the separation from our family, was preparing us for the good things that lay ahead, namely being reunited with everyone. But this was a necessary step, as painful as it was. That also taught me to see the big picture, to understand that some sacrifices are for the greater good. And yet, even in tough times one had to find the good and to appreciate every little good thing that came our way.

I learned to really and truly count my blessings every single day. I also learned how to see the big picture.

Age and experience led me to think that my father probably was feeling sad and lonely when we were living in Spain, but he put on a good face for my benefit. He wanted me to be strong so I could get through the tough times. He wanted me to see the positive in everything. Being able to do that is a great gift. I inherited from my dad the ability to live in the moment and not worry needlessly about a future you can't control. The key word here is *needlessly*. If there's good cause to be concerned, I'll worry, whereas my father was nonchalant in the extreme. Living for the moment, well, he raised that to an art form.

I agree with him that the present is the most important thing. I don't know what's going to happen tonight, but I know what's happening right now. You can plan for the future but what you live is the moment.

My father's greatest asset was his personality. He was so *simpático*. I can't think of a better word to describe him. It went far beyond just charm. He was sincere; he was warm; he was carefree, open, and affectionate. He had an infectious laugh and he put people at ease immediately. I don't think he ever met a person he didn't like, and I'm pretty sure anyone who met him liked him immediately. Even now, several years after his death, people who knew him only slightly smile at the mention of his name.

Speaking of his name, he never went by Emilio, which was his given name. He was known to one and all as Capetillo. Emilio Capetillo was a character in a very popular radio show in Cuba called *Los Tres Villalobos*. Emilio Capetillo was the bad guy, "*el terror de los Villalobos*," the villain, always trying to trip them up. Nothing could be farther from the type of guy my father was, but someone dubbed him "Capetillo" after the character and the name stuck.

There was always a special bond between my father and me and it only grew stronger during our time in Spain. I always felt a real affinity for him and I never got annoyed at him or expected him to be anything or anyone besides himself. In Spain, when I began to feel that I was the grown-up and he was the kid, I just let him be and never judged him. I'd just lived through the traumatic experience of leaving my country, my family, and everything I'd ever known behind and headed into the unknown. That left a profound impression on me in so many ways. I am my father's son, and I say that with great pride and affection. But the circumstances of life have a formative effect on you—how could it be otherwise? I was determined to take the best parts of my father's personality—his generosity, his cheerful attitude—and meld them with attributes that I figured I would need to survive and to thrive in this life.

Most of all I adopted his positive outlook. I prefer to stack the odds in my favor by working hard and planning, but he taught me the value of looking on the bright side. By the time we left Spain it was like a reflex to me, and it's served me well my whole life.

CHAPTER THREE

Define Your Own Success

T he definition of success is different for everyone. For one person success could be coming home at three o'clock in the afternoon and playing ball with his kids. Someone else might want to clean shoes four hours a day and spend the rest of her time surfing or lying on the beach staring at the ocean. Other people skip that and work till nine o'clock so they can send their kids to a great school. Another person might not rest until he can afford to buy a whole baseball team for himself, but I'm not like that. I split it in half: I work during the week and dedicate the weekends to my family. Also I get up in the morning and cook for my daughter and take her to school. The important lesson is that I've decided what I need to do to feel satisfied: I've defined my own success.

A lot of people push themselves hard, working really long hours, but they don't have any goal in sight. What do you need to be successful? Money? Some people don't care about money. They want to live in peace. Perhaps you want a job with flexible vacation time and good pay so you can travel. Or you want to send your kids to college, which is getting more and more expensive every year. If you've figured it out, and you can pull it off and be happy and make it work, then you're successful.

Again I think back to my father, the person who was my most important role model when I was growing up. My father never had a lot of material things, nor was he an acquisitive man. Even having a family didn't motivate him beyond working to get what was needed and not much more. Saving and planning for the future were never priorities for him. Nor was my dad much of a businessman, even though he came from a long line of entrepreneurs. (Looking at my grandfather and his success in the textiles business, I think perhaps the entrepreneurial gene skips a generation.)

My father's parents were originally from Lebanon, a small country in the Middle East that has produced an incredible number of entrepreneurs over the centuries. My grandparents had a marriage arranged by their two families. At the time my grandfather Jalin was in his forties and my grandmother Julia was barely in her teens. After their marriage, which took place in Africa, where my grandmother's family lived, they went first to France and then on to Cuba, where they settled. My grandfather was a very successful businessman and he made a fortune many times over. He had an amazing business sense, and imported merchandise, sold textiles, and did extremely well for himself and his family of twelve children.

But one day, in a business dispute, someone pulled a gun on my grandfather and shot and killed him. My grandmother was left with twelve children and no way to support herself. She hardly spoke Spanish. My grandfather had money, but as was the custom in those days, he didn't talk to his wife about the business and finances. But there was the merchandise, the textiles, and the cloth he had in stock, along with some jewelry he'd given her, and my grandmother was able to sell it to support the family for a while.

My father wasn't even a teenager when his own father died and he became a door-to-door salesman. He sold soap, razor blades, toiletries, brushes, combs, gels, dyes, cleaning supplies, things like this. I still remember him rattling off the list of goods he used to sell, like an auctioneer.

Going to work meant the end of my father's formal education. There wasn't money for him to stay in school, and his family needed everyone to contribute their share. As far as my father was concerned, the greatest school in the world is the street. This was a phrase he repeated often. If the streets are the best place to get an education, as he believed, then he got a PhD. In some ways, he was right: I've known people with numerous degrees who have no street (or even common!) sense.

At some point, while attending this "school" on the streets, my father learned to play cards. He found that not only was he good at cards, he was lucky, and it soon became his trade. He was in his teens when he became a professional cardplayer. There wasn't any stigma attached to earning your living that way. Gambling and games of chance were very much a part of Cuban culture. In fact, gambling was legal in Cuba until Fidel outlawed it and closed the casinos. Until then people came from all over to play there, a lot like they do in Las Vegas nowadays.

For my father, playing cards was his job, and it was a job he enjoyed enormously. He cared very little about his winnings; the idea was simply to make enough to stay in the game. That's how he defined success. But his gaming skills didn't help us much when we were in Spain. He never played cards there, and since he wasn't allowed to work, he never made any money all the time we were in the country.

While life was tough in Spain my father never allowed it to be grim. It was what it was, and we were going to make the best of it and find joy in the little things. To my father, there was much more to life than just getting by. We're here to enjoy it. Something I have often seen in very rich people—and I know plenty of people who have a lot of money—is that they don't really enjoy life. I do. This is another thing I inherited from my father—the decision to enjoy life, all the time. I live every day to the max; I live every day as if it were my last.

I am a lot like him in that I'm not attached to money or to possessions. From him I learned what the real values are in life: The simple things are the ones that you enjoy the most. I can be carefree like him. I know only too well how life can change in an instant. I enjoy hugging my children, my friends. I love to spend time with my family and have fun with the people I work with. The moment that passes does not come back. But I'm a lot more practical than he was. I like to plan and I'm very goal oriented, perhaps not in spite of him but because of him. My father's ways and his joie de vivre made me laugh, but they also made me more aware of the need to be responsible. His laughter kept us going when things were rough, but I have mixed that with the security that comes from attaining goals and looking toward the future.

As you plan and move forward your definition of success might well change. You've been planning to send your kids to college. What happens when they graduate? Perhaps you'll start planning for a comfortable retirement. When I left Cuba I had one goal, and that was to reunite my family. Once I'd succeeded in that goal I lived for another priority: that my kids should never have to go through what I went through.

Changing your definition of success has a lot to do with motivation, which we'll discuss in the next chapter. It's also connected to inspiration, which is different again. Perhaps we're looking at the same thing three different ways! But what's important is that you're aware of your own attitude. You can have a kind of running conversation with yourself. Am I succeeding in realizing my goals? Can I keep doing this for the rest of my working life? What do I need to do to make a change? And what *are* my goals, anyway?

The ultimate measure of success, and maybe what you really want to achieve, is being able to share what you have with the people you love, providing for their needs and also for their wants. One day when we were all living in Miami I got a huge bill from the dentist. I figured out quickly it was because of my dad, and I asked him how he spent so much money at the dentist. He admitted he'd been sending people he knew over there to have their teeth fixed on my tab. In the end I guess it was a win for both of us. My dad succeeded in getting his friends' teeth fixed. And I was providing for my dad—my family.

And success is in the simple joys. When I watch my daughter playing, it makes me so happy. My childhood was hardly carefree. I think it is good to reflect on these things so you can understand the drive for success.

To me success is also doing something positive and creative. I've found success in the business world working with wonderfully creative people. It's hard to separate the man from the businessman. Perhaps it's impossible. Your company or your business will be a reflection of who you are. Your values will imbue your business and inspire those who work for and with you.

People who become successful or achieve a new level of power and who change their personalities aren't on the right track. Don't let success change you. Do the right thing, always. You'll feel good about it, even if it's hard. This is important to remember. When you have achieved your dreams, and you are successful by your own standards, don't change. Be real, and continue to be original. And keep that positive personality and outlook we talked about already.

CHAPTER FOUR

Motivate!

I just talked about defining success. How do you see your own life right now? As interesting as it might be to find out how someone else has lived and found success, you need to look at yourself and examine your own situation, your values and lifestyle, so you can be in a position to start carrying out your own goals.

First things first. It's critically important that you determine what really motivates you. There's a difference between *motivation* and *inspiration*. Motivation is much more pressing and immediate than inspiration. Motivation is what gets you out of bed in the morning—inspiration might be what comes to you when you are hanging out on a golden beach somewhere. I'm exaggerating, but only to make a point: Motivation is a necessity, inspiration more of a luxury. Put it this way: If you're not motivated, you're never going to be in a position to get inspired!

Of course, motivation is about more than the basic incentives of life, and inspiration is more than simply reaching for clever ideas born of a great feeling. Prayer is often described as "talking" and meditation as "listening." It is an interesting distinction, and we could use it to describe the difference between motivation and inspiration. We're motivated first by need and later by desire, and we are inspired by something greater still. Motivation and inspiration—put simply, one moves the body and the other fills the soul.

Motivation is the expression ("talking") of what you want to do and to achieve. Inspiration involves a great deal of listening, beginning with yourself.

Think of motivation as movement. It is motion; it is action. Motivation involves a lot of get-up-and-go. It is the fuel that moves you to carry things out. Motivation comes from need, primarily, and some needs are extremely basic—food, warmth, shelter—while some are much deeper—a sense of worth and purpose, kindness, companionship, love. Defining for yourself the combination of the basic needs and the deeper needs will help you understand your motivation so you can put it to better use for yourself.

Having said all that, it might be the case that you are happy with your current situation, whatever that might be. If so, then keep doing what you're doing. You may have reached the height of your ambition—you're exactly as motivated as you need to be. That's great. Some people's ambitions are limited. If you don't have any money and you stay in bed all day and that's okay with you, then you can be sure nothing good is going to happen to you. It's about *dreams*. A few, a very lucky few, have realized their dreams. Most of us have unfulfilled ambitions that require we get up and go in search of them. In order to do that we need to remember our motivation.

LET'S BEGIN WITH THE BASICS. No matter how tired I am, no matter how late I got to bed the night before, and no matter where I am in the world, I always feel motivated to get an early start on my day. When I say early, I mean five o'clock. I get up early in part out of habit. But there is also a need—a need to get things done—and I have never felt that there is enough time in the day to tackle all the things I want to do.

I am motivated by this basic, practical need. I have to be perpetually in motion, doing things, creating, achieving. At this point in my life this fundamental motivation is all I need. You may be at a stage where the key is that you need to work to make money in order to take care of your family and yourself. It's the bottom line. You also need to work because doing nothing is soul-destroying. Everyone loves a vacation, but there are very few people who could tolerate lying on a beach 365 days a year. I know I couldn't. We all need meaning in our lives, and work well-done is something that we can all find fulfilling. Simple, basic motivation.

As I see it, no matter how much you love something, enthusiasm does wane from time to time. Maybe you're tired; maybe you're bored with what you're doing; maybe you're frustrated because things aren't going the way you want or they're not moving forward as quickly as you'd hoped they would. So you always need a reason to keep at it even if you are truly doing what you want to do.

To find that reason, ask yourself what really gets you up and going, and what will keep you going for the long haul. Sometimes you need only a small boost to get in gear. An eleventh-hour deadline can provide powerful, albeit short-term, motivation.

The chance to earn easy money is another example of a potent motivator or, more accurately speaking, an incentive. There is nothing wrong with this kind of motivation, but it's often the case that the opportunities and the rewards that come with it are fairly limited. You get the nice one-off job that pays you a decent chunk of change, but once that's done, you're back to the grind. When that happens, you need to have a reason to be doing what you are doing and you can't lose sight of that reason. When you've figured out just what it is that motivates you, you will begin to see what inspires you and leads you to greater heights.

In order to understand your own motivation beyond need, you have to do some serious soul-searching. You need to review your values. What do you believe in, and how do you go about putting those beliefs into practice? You are figuring out who you are. You have to define your own life and really and truly know who you are, without masks, without pretense, without any of the walls you might put up between you and the world. Do this first with yourself and it will be so much easier to be authentic with others.

So many people are unable to move toward realizing their dreams because they fail to think clearly about who they are. To me it's important to adopt an attitude of gratitude. Think about everything you have to be thankful for—your health, your family, your job, your country. For some people, this is easier than for others, but everyone can humble themselves just a little and say, "I am grateful," or "I am blessed," or even "I'm just so lucky."

So, count your blessings—literally: your material as well as your spiritual ones. In doing this you will be guided by two things: your conscience and God. If you ever feel you are doing something wrong, you probably are—your conscience can't be wrong. But I think more than anything, karma is important. Whatever goodness you have in your heart will come back to you. And whatever hatred, that too will come back at you.

After you have given thanks or put yourself in a mind-set where you feel gratitude (whether to God, the higher power, or just plain old Lady Luck), think of all that you have. Do you have a roof over your head? Plenty of people don't, maybe because they are poor, they have fallen on hard times, or they are refugees. Be grateful if you have somewhere safe to live, no matter how humble. Are you healthy? That's a big plus. I get up in the morning and just feel so grateful that I can do it all by myself. Plenty of people can't. Count yourself lucky. Are you doing what you like? Well, that's what this book is all about, so if you aren't doing what you like, you soon will be. If you are doing what you like, you are indeed very, very fortunate.

Don't just think about yourself: Is your family healthy? There is nothing more upsetting than a loved one's illness, or nothing more challenging than the disability of a loved one, be it a parent, a partner, or a child. Again, count yourself lucky.

Counting blessings and being grateful are part of having the generally positive attitude that I've said is fundamental to success in life. This is where it slots into the bigger picture. It doesn't matter what kind of person you are; a positive attitude is going to get you a lot farther than a negative one. Even when I had very little, I was happy to have what I had. I didn't complain about my situation; I went out to try to improve it. Again and again we'll return to this theme: Think positive! Even when you aren't feeling especially motivated, thinking positive will get you back on track.

All of this introspection inevitably makes us think of our place in the world, and spirituality or religion. I was brought up Catholic but I don't profess any one religion anymore. I believe that all religions have something to offer and that we can learn something from each and every one of them. I do believe in a higher power and a higher purpose, and I believe we have to be kind to one another, help one another out, and always strive to do and be our best. And to top it all off, we have to be grateful for all that we have, all that we have done, and all we are capable of doing. That's my creed, no more, no less.

What motivates you on a day-to-day basis might change over the course of your life, but for me the foundation has remained the same. It's always been and continues to be family. Everything else, important as it might be, is secondary. As a teenager I was motivated both by lack of opportunity—when the Communist government in Cuba cracked down on all freedoms—and also by opportunity, the chance to go to the United States and to really live my life fully and in freedom.

I first felt the drive and motivation during the several-year period when my life and the lives of my family members changed so dramatically. More than anything else, my original motivation to succeed came from having to face at a very early age the reality of the life that lay ahead for my family and me. When communism came to Cuba, it changed the country totally. It changed our way of life and it would change our future.

Young as I was I felt I had to do something for all of my family, because we could not risk being stuck in that system for years on end. But what choice did we have at that point? We were such a close family, and yet I knew that our salvation lay in our separation. Perhaps I could leave the country and try to bring them all with me—eventually. I decided that my leaving was our only hope. I knew that if I did, my God, we might never all be together again. This was a terrible, heartbreaking possibility. But the thought of condemning all of us to a life under communism was worse still.

I knew that I might never see my family again, but I also knew that this was the only decision that I could have made. It was the most important decision of my life. From that moment on my determination to reunite my family was all the motivation I needed. I still feel the same drive even though the circumstances have changed. And I constantly tap into those memories and the feelings they provoke to push myself forward. Those same memories and feelings are also part of what inspire me, something which is probably still more complex than motivation.

My enthusiasm and my passion for whatever I am doing are tremendous motivations. Another motivation is the desire to do and to complete. It is great to dream and then to talk, but ultimately you need to follow through and finish what you start.

It won't be hard for you to figure out your motivation. Some are motivated by opportunity—their parents sacrificed and gave them a great education—while others are motivated by a lack of opportunity. Sometimes it is a dramatic event, like the death of a parent, or a family's hard luck, that changes your life and helps to determine the path you follow. The way you go down that path, however, is your choice.

CHAPTER FIVE

Be Open to Change

I t is human nature to fear change. But have you ever noticed how sudden dramatic change can present the greatest opportunities in life? Be open to change and the new things it provides. The biggest change in our lives—leaving our homeland—provided all of my family with its greatest opportunity—living in the United States, living in freedom. And leaving Cuba was just the beginning of so much change. And of so much opportunity.

It's 1968. I am fifteen and, with my father, Emilio Sr., I have been living in Spain for eighteen months since we left our beloved homeland in Cuba. My mother and my older brother are still on the island and we're all desperate to reunite the family. In fact, the family is about to become farther apart than ever, because I've been granted a student visa to travel to the United States. I'm heading for Miami, where my uncle and aunt live. This is going to be only a temporary separation: Our dream is that soon we'll all be living together, as free citizens of the United States.

For generations, families trying to move to this country have been forced to split up, with the head of the household, the father, traveling ahead of everyone else to establish a foothold. My family is going about it a little differently. I'm the youngest and I'm blazing the trail for the rest of my family. As soon as I can I'll petition for my father to join me, and then we'll be able to bring everyone together at last.

I should mention here something that took place in Spain that scared me. A few days before we left Cuba, I started to feel sharp pains in my abdomen, and when we got to Spain there was a very noticeable and uncomfortable bump there. I had no idea what it could be, and because we had no money for a doctor I just had to live with the occasional discomfort. Soon, however, the pain became worse, and my father found a charity hospital willing to take a look at me. The doctor determined that I had a hernia. He said it wasn't going to get better on its own and I needed an operation. I was frightened by the idea of surgery, especially since we didn't have any other family close by to help us out when I recovered. But my father insisted that I have the operation so that I would be well again and not in near-constant pain.

The day arrived for the surgery, and my father checked me into the hospital in the late afternoon and left me there. He wasn't allowed to stay with me or even to come in past the reception desk. I had to go in all by myself. I would have to spend the night there to be prepared for the surgery the next morning. I had to fast the night before the surgery and couldn't eat or drink after ten o'clock at night.

A charity hospital is not a pretty place, and it scared me. I felt a wave of loneliness wash over me. The room I was in was a large, open ward shared by what seemed like dozens of people. It was noisy and stuffy, and you could hear everything everyone said, the moaning and crying and generally the sounds of human misery. There was someone in a bed nearby who was dying. I knew it because a priest came to administer the last rites. I decided I wasn't going to stick around. In the middle of the night I sneaked out of bed and took my clothes out of the drawer where I'd left them. I dressed and folded the hospital gown and left it neatly on the bed. Then I walked quietly out of the hospital and walked home.

When I reached home I went and hid in the bathtub. I thought my dad was going to kill me. First thing next morning the police were at the door looking for my father. The hospital realized I wasn't where I was supposed to be and they came looking for me.

Was my father surprised to see me? Probably not. And we did not discuss the incident further. Clearly, this was my decision, and my father wasn't going to force me to have the surgery. I would just have to live with the discomfort until either I could face the surgery or the pain became too much. I was willing to live with the consequences of my actions, and for my father that was good enough.

My father and I never intended to stay in Spain and make a life for ourselves there. It was a place of transition, and we were grateful for the refuge. The worst part of the waiting was that it was open-ended. We were never told by any official at the U.S. Embassy if our visas would take six months, a year, or longer. They had no way of knowing, and there were plenty of people in line ahead of us. The other factor was money, because a relative in the United States generally had to show that he could support the person he was petitioning for. And we were not the only relatives my aunt Javivi and my uncle Pepe were trying to get out of Cuba and into the United States.

Finally, the day came. Eighteen months after our arrival in Madrid I was granted my student visa to enter the United States. My father would not be able to go with me right away. The plan was for me to go ahead and petition for him. As a minor, I believe I was given some kind of priority to be reunited with a parent.

Again, my aunt Javivi had sent money for my ticket. I can only imagine how hard she worked for that money, and how much she had sacrificed and saved. To this day, I shake my head in wonder at her generosity. I knew instinctively, though, that there wasn't much that I would be able to do for her. The only way I could repay her was to do what she had done for me for others. And I knew my chance would come very soon to do just that.

After a year and a half in Spain I was able to join family members in Miami. I was ready to learn a new language. I was excited at the thought of what lay ahead. Even though the United States would be even more different than Spain was, I was energized by the thought of change. The tough economic times in Spain were quickly replaced by the many opportunities our new country offered us. The streets of Miami weren't paved with gold. I never believed they were. And I was ready to roll up my sleeves and work to achieve that dream of getting my mother and brother out of Cuba. I was so grateful for that opportunity and I remain grateful for it to this day.

It's extraordinary how vividly we can remember these life-changing scenes in our lives. As if it were only yesterday, as the saying goes. This day, the day I moved to the United States, absolutely stands out for me. My father took me to the airport in Madrid, and, before our final good-bye, he handed me a couple of bottles of cognac, a gift for a friend in the United States who had also occasionally sent us money while we were in Spain. What a different departure this was from the time I had left Cuba! I did not feel that overwhelming, almost paralyzing sense of sadness I had experienced when I said good-bye to my mother and brother. Instead, I felt free and I felt so very hopeful. Even though I was leaving my father, my journey to America meant we were one step closer to realizing the dream of reuniting our family.

As the plane began its approach into New York's Kennedy airport I could barely contain my excitement. Hours before, I'd given up trying to sleep on the long flight. Whatever nervousness I had was far outweighed by the excitement I felt about going to the United States. To me the world seemed full of promise. During the eighteen months I had spent in Spain, I had matured years. I felt confident that I could face whatever lay ahead. I knew there were great opportunities for me and for all of my family in America. I was comforted by the idea of joining my aunt and uncle and other family members who had gotten out of Cuba and were now also living in Miami. I knew that in my aunt's home there was a lot of love and affection and I was so looking forward to rejoining my extended family. I had missed them all so very much.

I got off the plane and went through customs and immigration without incident. Once I was through customs I had to find my connecting flight, and I didn't know how to ask where my gate was. I just kept saying, "Miami? Miami?" and eventually someone pointed me to the gate. Once I knew where I was supposed to be, I was almost giddy with excitement. I wasn't scared anymore.

Successful immigrants often talk about arriving to this country with only the clothes on their backs and a couple of dollars in their pockets. In my case, it's true that I really didn't have any money or possessions to speak of when I arrived at Kennedy airport. But what I did have with me was worth so much more than a suitcase full of clothes and a nicely stuffed wallet. None of what I brought with me could be measured or quantified.

I arrived in this country with an extraordinary sense of optimism about the future. I was going to be free and nothing could stop me. I also carried with me an unbending willingness to work hard. If I had to I'd labor all the hours God gave me. I'd be happy to work, because I knew that was how I would make progress in this country. I was certain I had a great many other attributes—ideas, enthusiasm, passion, drive— but the foundations on which I was going to build my new life were hope and hard work. All I needed was the opportunity. As soon as I got here I couldn't wait to get started. Back in 1968, that excited kid did make it to Miami in one piece. (But I never did meet up with my father's friend to give him the bottles of cognac I carried from Spain. I still have the bottles to this day.)

That fifteen-year-old kid who arrived at Kennedy airport did not enjoy an unbroken succession of triumphs as he made his way through life in America. Not by any means. On any number of occasions I've been told that I couldn't do something. At first, I was too young. It seemed like very little time passed before I was informed I was too old to learn new skills. Early on, my lack of English was an obstacle. I have been too Hispanic for some purposes and not Hispanic enough for others. Even as I achieved success in business I have been met with negativity: You can't invest in that neighborhood; you can't hire that person; nobody wants to listen to that kind of music. Anyone who knows me will confirm—don't tell me I can't do it. Saying no is like issuing a challenge to me, and I will always look for a way to turn a negative into a positive.

It's not just me. My whole family lives life with this spirit and attitude. No single event in my life has inspired me more than watching my beautiful wife, Gloria, walk again after doctors told her it would never happen following her devastating accident in 1990. Don't tell Gloria she can't either.

I know that if I'd stayed in Cuba my life would have been one of dead ends and frustration. In that country no means no. I am eternally grateful to the United States for giving me the opportunities I enjoyed here. That statement is no less true for being a cliché. In the United States, where I was free, I always found a way to make it happen. I knew when I reached America that I would have a chance to succeed on my own terms. Change is rarely easy, I agree. But if you decide to face it head-on, you can more easily embrace the opportunities change brings.

CHAPTER SIX

Find Your Advantage

Y ou may feel in your professional life that you are being discriminated against. You need to be careful of making assumptions like that. Sometimes we are treated in a certain way because we are
different. We live in a very diverse society, and we are all richer for it.
But people can be fearful, envious, ignorant of that which is different.

I can almost count on one hand the times I was truly discriminated
against because of my country of origin. Most of the time being who I
am, and coming from where I do, has been a great advantage. And when
it hasn't necessarily been an advantage, I've learned to turn it into one.

Immigrants. So many of us come to this country with a ferocious desire and drive to succeed. When immigrants sailed to this country in
huge numbers in the nineteenth century, millions of them looked out for
the Statue of Liberty in New York Harbor, the landmark that showed
they'd reached their promised land. For these people Lady Liberty sym-
bolized hope. Hope is the great currency of the immigrant, and its value
is incalculable. And it was when I had nothing that I was the most full
of hope.

The immigrant has almost inexhaustible reserves of hope. We've
thought about the American dream since the moment we decided we
wanted to live in this country, and we'll do anything to achieve it. Of
course, that doesn't mean we abandon our culture and heritage the min-

ute we set foot in the United States. I am very proud of who I am and where I'm from. It's great not only to maintain your culture but to share it with others. Americans are obviously very open to that. They have accepted and embraced traditions from the world over. Don't underestimate how open people can be to trying new things.

I have always used my language and my culture to my advantage. Our music is a great example. My entire career is based on who I am and where I come from. Along the way, I have had to deal with my fair share of narrow-minded people because of it. On a personal level, that was hard. But again, I persisted and fought through the obstacles.

I remember years ago traveling by plane with my son, Nayib. We weren't seated together—I was in one row and Nayib was right behind me. It was very unfortunate, because that day Nayib was having an asthma attack and he had just taken some medication to ward it off. The pills he took made him slightly hyper, not a very comfortable situation for a ten-year-old boy traveling by plane.

I was settling into my seat, with my ticket in my hand, when the flight attendant approached me. She asked me if I would mind moving, because there was a group of three people who all wanted to sit together. I said, "I don't mind at all as long as I can be seated near my son, because he is having an asthma attack." Instead of trying to accommodate what I think anyone would consider a reasonable request, all of a sudden, the flight attendant got annoyed and said very rudely, "Get up. You have to move." I showed her my ticket but she just continued to insist that I get out of my seat. And her tone changed. I began to feel she was treating me badly because I was different, obviously "foreign." I was right, because after I said, no, I wouldn't move without my son, she said, "Why don't you just go back to where you came from?"

I remained calm, even though her comment stung me. I told her that what she was doing was wrong. She didn't seem to care. I then asked her for her name. I didn't raise hell; I didn't name-call. I wasn't even tempted to. I firmly told her that I was a customer and as such I had my rights. And I wasn't going to move—not now, anyway. I stayed put, close to my son.

I later sent a letter to the airline, and within two weeks I received a very courteous response from the chairman of the company, apologizing. The woman who had mistreated me had been temporarily suspended. (Apparently, this had not been her first offense!) I didn't want her fired. I wanted her to understand that she had treated me badly for no reason. That needed to be communicated to her. Maybe she had had a bad day, but it was a horrible thing to say, and I was certainly within my rights.

I knew I was right not to confront her directly because I wasn't going to get anywhere, and besides, it would have just ended very unpleasantly. If I've learned anything along the way, there really are three magic words in dealing with other human beings: please, sorry, thanks. We don't use them enough.

For all the stories of discrimination and rejection that I can recount, there are a hundred positive experiences that I can repeat. No, make that several million, judging from our record sales over the years! That is the true indicator of acceptance in this country for us. The American audience has been receptive and welcoming of a different sound and a different culture.

And that is what I focus on.

A LOT OF TIMES, IMMIGRANTS bring their own ways to this country and assume that institutions in the United States operate in the same way as they do where we came from. Be careful of assumptions. For instance, if you think you have been denied a loan because of your country of origin, make sure that you didn't actually forget to fill out all the papers correctly, or you didn't forget to bring all the necessary documentation. Maybe you have no credit history or maybe you have bad credit. Those are things that with some effort and discipline you can correct.

Remember that sometimes we don't get what we want, or feel we deserve, because we really aren't qualified or we didn't proceed correctly. Do things right the first time and don't be too quick to make judgments. Learn to follow the rules and laws of this country and whatever country you work and do business in. But also remember that you do have rights, and the most basic of those rights is to be treated fairly and with respect.

If your name is difficult to pronounce, be patient. Help the person who is trying to pronounce your name. However, if you're a customer and you really feel you're not being treated with respect because of your ethnic origin, ask to speak to a supervisor. Don't cause a scandal—what's the point? The person who is mistreating you obviously doesn't get it, but perhaps his or her supervisor could explain it more effectively than you can. Let the supervisor know that you feel you are being treated poorly but, again, arm yourself with facts. There are laws in this country that protect people against discrimination. And just as we are willing to respect the laws of this land, we are entitled to protection by those laws. Know your rights.

When you're making a fresh start, whether it's moving to a new country, or starting a new business or a new job, you will have moments when you feel that you are at the bottom of the heap. Starting all over, even at the bottom, can be a great opportunity. It can make you more understanding and compassionate. If you've been handed everything in life you simply don't have the same motivation to strive and cover your basic needs and those of your family. But when you have had difficult circumstances, it is pretty easy to understand what it is to walk in the other guy's shoes. Necessity is a great motivator.

That's why so many immigrants achieve such great success. They have the fire inside. It's another important part of the immigrant advantage. Being an immigrant helped me to be aggressive, and persistent not only about money but about life. There are a lot of people in positions of power and influence who don't have a lot of contact with what is really happening on the streets, with what is really going on in the world. Coming from the bottom up, starting a new business and starting out on your own, can be great experiences for you, if you let them be.

As I said before, I think Latinos moving to this country now have certain advantages I didn't enjoy in the late sixties. The market is more receptive to Latino products and ideas, which means it's easier to bring over applicable elements from your home culture to this country.

That was always something I worked hard to do. Cuban music was what I knew, so I worked with the sounds I was familiar with, whether it was playing the accordion for tips in a restaurant or producing a record for a platinum-disc-selling artist later on. In the same way, when we had the opportunity to open a restaurant, I never considered doing anything other than Cuban food—which we did when we opened Bongos Cuban Café.

I know that there's a whole generation of Cuban kids who've never visited the island. Enough time has passed that there are maybe even two generations. Their exposure to Cuban music and Cuban food—Cuban culture in general—can be pretty limited. We have to work to keep alive the traditions we brought with us from our homeland. It's very important for me to try to defend my heritage and to remember where I came from. It's also meant that what I've done hasn't been American cookie-cutter. I've always had something different to offer.

All the time we have to defend ourselves against caricatures and stereotypes. Our Latino culture isn't about hot tamales. I remember at an award show once they wanted to dress Gloria up in an outfit with fruit on it, like Carmen Miranda. We might be immigrants but we are not stereotypes. Immigrants deserve to be treated with respect.

The experience of being an immigrant has very definitely contributed to my approach to life. I still have an immigrant mentality, even though I have spent more time in this country than I ever did in Cuba. The African-American, Asian-American, and Latino communities do a lot for this country. All immigrant communities do a lot. We are all contributing economically, culturally, in the war effort, in all areas of life. We know it but we sometimes have to remind the larger community of our contributions. I am both awed and humbled by the contributions of immigrants to this country. And I define immigrants pretty broadly—children and grandchildren of immigrants have made tremendous strides for their families and in their communities and have made enormous contributions. How often have you heard of someone who is running a huge corporation whose grandparents came from elsewhere or had very humble beginnings? (And remember, our president is also the son of an immigrant.)

Those of us who are immigrants—not all Latinos are immigrants; many have been here for generations—haven't come to take jobs away from Americans. We have come to contribute and to help continue to build this great country, a country that we love and are loyal to, whether or not we were born here.

Find your own advantage. It might well involve many of the same attributes I have outlined as part of my immigrant experience. Taking pride in who you are, where you are from (your cultural background, family, school, work experience, interests and hobbies, special abilities) are all part of your advantage. Identify your differences, your abilities, and celebrate them, and use them to your advantage.

CHAPTER SEVEN

Honor Your Family

I have been extraordinarily blessed to be part of two wonderful families in my life. I was born into the family created by my mother and father. Later I enjoyed the amazing good fortune of making my own family with my wife, Gloria, and our children, Nayib and Emily, and with my extended family, most especially with my mother-in-law, Gloria Fajardo, who over the years has become another mother to me. Surround yourself with family and work on those relationships. Commit to them, be loyal to them, take pride in them. The only people who are really always going to be there to celebrate your successes, and console you in your failures, are your family members.

It all starts with the family. It's impossible to overstate how important family is to me. Everything that I and Estefan Enterprises are today begins and ends with my family. For me, family has been a great source of strength and support.

Families are always changing, of course. Older relatives from our first family leave us; younger ones get married and add new branches to their own family tree. But the presence of the family is a constant whenever we look at it.

I look back at my childhood and all my memories are focused on my first family.

In my best memory of childhood I am diving into the warm turquoise water of the Caribbean, floating to the top and lying there as still as I can, simply luxuriating in the moment. The sun is shining, waves are lapping the beach, and I don't have a care in the world, not a single one. It's a perfect summer's day that I recall, and I'm blissfully happy and full of energy. The entire day I'm running in and out of the water or I'm at the water's edge playing in the sand. I stop only when my grandmother or my mother insists I come out of the water to have something to eat.

Not every day of my childhood was as carefree as this, of course. One summer when I was about eight years old I fell deathly ill. All of a sudden I developed a high fever that just kept climbing. I don't remember much other than being sent to bed and being made to stay there. I was a pretty energetic kid—these days you'd say I was hyper—so keeping me quiet would normally have been a lot of work for my mother and grandmother, who looked after me most of the time. But on this occasion I was so sick I don't think I put up much of a fight.

Most of my memories of those days are now a blur. But what I know is that my family took good care of me. I can close my eyes and remember feeling my mother gently rubbing my hand, putting cool towels on my forehead. I can hear her soft and soothing voice. I was sick for a long time, maybe even a matter of weeks, before the fever broke. And when it did, it left me very weak.

My condition was serious enough that my grandmother insisted we leave the city and go to La Socapa, a small island not far from our home in Santiago, where I could recover. My grandmother thought that since my defenses were low, it would be better to keep me isolated and away from other people and potential sources of infection. She also said that being out of the humidity of the city and near the ocean air would cure me and make me strong. And sure enough, soon after getting to the island, I was running around again, full of energy. My grandmother was right—not only was I better; I was happy, really happy.

La Socapa was just a ferry ride from our home in the city of Santiago, Cuba's second-biggest city, in the eastern province of Oriente. After my illness, we started to spend all our holidays and vacations, sometimes even weekends, in La Socapa. It was warm, colorful, and bright, and I felt like a little island boy, hanging out on the beach building sand castles and climbing trees, and floating in the crystal water. Getting sick was a good thing, I figured, since after that I got to spend so much time in our own little paradise.

The days spent on my magical island made up one of the few truly carefree periods in my childhood. My early years were full of family and warmth, but hanging over everything I remember a nagging feeling that something bad was going to happen. By the time I started school, the revolution was in full swing and people were starting to leave Cuba in droves. Some people had left even just before Castro took power. They could see what lay ahead and didn't like it. In any case, staying or going was the constant topic of conversation for most family gatherings for a long time.

I WAS BORN IN SANTIAGO de Cuba on March 4, 1953, the year that marked the real beginning of the Cuban Revolution. This was an event that, when it came to fruition in 1959, would force us to leave our home and divide my family for years. I was too little to be aware of the details of what was happening during those early years, but I knew during my entire childhood that things weren't right with the world; at least, they weren't right in the world as it existed outside our front door. Away from the house, life was always much more complicated. I remember a powerful sense of uncertainty. And that uncertainty crept into our lives and threatened our happy and close life together.

The city of Santiago is in eastern Cuba. Because of its size and location it played a key role in the revolution. University students and workers who hated the Batista regime mounted an urban resistance in Santiago and joined forces with Fidel Castro's group after a failed attempt to overthrow the government in 1953. Our city felt the effects of the revolution even as it was just starting to develop. And it was here, from a balcony in Santiago's city hall, that Castro announced his force's victory and the arrival of the revolution on January 1, 1959. I was not yet six years old.

We lived in a large house in the Carretera del Morro section of Santiago, close to family and to school, and with lots of friends in the neighborhood—the usual familiar things of childhood. I lived there with my mother and father, together with grandparents—my mother's parents—my older brother, and one of my mother's two brothers. We easily fit into that spacious house, since it ran the length of almost an entire city block and it had at least seven bedrooms. From the front door in, our home lives were pretty comfortable and happy. We never had a lot of material wealth—despite the size of the house, we weren't wealthy—but we had one another and that always seemed to be enough.

My mother's parents, Antonio Gomez and Carmen Vasquez, had emigrated from Spain before my mother was born. Antonio, born in La Coruña in Spain, made his living in Santiago first with a greengrocer's store and later buying and selling land and real estate. He soon built up his business and lived comfortably, able to provide well for my grandmother, my mother, and her two brothers, although they never became genuinely wealthy. Back then, real estate was a good way to make a living, not a means to make a fortune. And that was fine by all of them.

My grandmother Carmen was a towering figure in our lives, literally and metaphorically. She was physically very tall, much taller than her husband, Antonio. Her role in the lives of her family was proportionate to her size, and she took care of everyone. Carmen had left her family behind in Galicia and had come to Cuba as part of a big wave of immigration from Spain at the turn of the twentieth century. She found work in Santiago with a wealthy and prominent family—the Bacardis, founders and owners of the famous rum company.

Carmen was working for the Bacardis when my grandfather met her and fell in love with her. Since Carmen's father had remained in Spain and she had no male relatives in Santiago, my grandfather asked Don Emilio Bacardi, the head of the family, for her hand in marriage. My grandmother was happy in her new country, in her marriage, and in the home she formed with Antonio. My grandparents had left Spain behind and found happiness and success in Cuba.

Both my parents—Emilio and Carmen—were born and raised in Santiago. They met, by chance, one day when my mother was in her early twenties and my father about twenty-six. They sat next to each other at a matinee in a theater and my father right away noticed her. He began to flirt with her by asking if he could borrow her fan. She lent it to him. And that was the beginning of a relationship that would last over sixty years.

Their backgrounds were quite different, both in terms of their cultures and their families. But that didn't stop them from getting married not long after they met. My father was very *simpático*, and sure of himself and of what he wanted. When he saw my mother, who was as beautiful as she was gentle, he saw a happy life ahead for the two of them.

But my mother's father, Antonio, wasn't so sure about Emilio. My father had no profession—"no visible means of support." He had been a door-to-door salesman when he was younger, until he became a professional cardplayer. He was managing to carve out a living for himself. My grandfather didn't believe that playing poker was a suitable profession for the husband of his daughter. "How is he going to make a living? How is he going to support a family?" my exasperated grandfather would say to my grandmother. But my father won over his future in-laws.

My brother, José, was born in 1945, the year after our parents married, and he had our mother and father pretty much all to himself until I came along eight years later. Because of the age difference, my brother and I didn't spend a lot of time together. He was already a boy when I was a baby, and by the time I was in school, Papo—my brother's nickname—was already in high school. But we were part of a warm, loving household and an even bigger tribe, so we have always been very close.

I have always thought that my parents' differences—different cultures, different types of families—gave my brother and me many advantages. I know the diversity of their backgrounds opened me up to be more interested in and more accepting of other cultures, and other people.

I do remember my grandfather's comings and goings. He kept the same schedule and kept it very strictly. He would come home for lunch at noon every day, and we were all expected to be there with him. And promptly at six in the evening, he would be home again to share the evening meal with all of us. The regularity of it was very reassuring. You could always count on my grandfather being there for our communal meals, and he could count on us to be there for him, as he wanted. My grandfather Antonio was the gentlest of men. He was a pleasure to be around, and his presence was always very comforting to all of us.

My father's widowed mother, Julia, and all eleven of his brothers and sisters also lived in Santiago. My father was the second-to-last in the family, and until his father's death when my dad was a child, they were a well-to-do family. My paternal grandfather, who was originally from Lebanon, was in the textiles trade and worked across Cuba and throughout the Caribbean. My father's older brothers all went into the same business or related clothing businesses in Santiago.

The family was pretty well-known, as much for its size as for its success, and the Estefans were a close-knit clan. The entire family got together often. After the revolution, when people started to worry openly about the future, the frequency of those gatherings increased. In fact, my grandmother Julia began to insist on seeing her children—and her children's children as well—every single day. (Fortunately her house was large enough to accommodate a constant flow of family visitors.)

Every evening, we would stop by my grandmother's house and visit with all the family. There were usually around seventy people there on any given evening. We would gather to see one another and to talk about the day. Usually nothing earth-shattering happened. The get-togethers were part of our routine. We would play cards or dominoes, the cousins would hang out together, sometimes we would eat a meal there, the adults would drink and laugh, and the tone would become serious only when the conversation turned to politics, something that began to happen more and more frequently.

As a young child, I spent most of my time with my mother and grandmother. (Nobody went to day care or preschool back then.) With my brother at school, I was the only child in the house most of the day, and I got accustomed to the company of women early on. My mother in particular had a very sweet nature, and I loved just being with her. I was in no rush to go to school, as I was quite content just hanging out at home. As for the company of kids my own age, I had friends in the neighborhood as well as the many cousins I saw all the time.

My mother was always my biggest cheerleader, and she was never critical of me.

She was completely focused on her family and gave us the sense that we could do anything we wanted and be whomever we wanted to be. From as early as I can remember right up to the day she died, that sense that anything was possible was certainly how I felt. I know I have that outlook because of my mother.

When my parents moved to this country I was determined to give something back to them. I bought a house for our family. Later, I bought a house for my parents and paid cash for it. They resisted the idea of owing money, which is why I didn't get a mortgage. When Gloria and I bought our house on Star Island in Miami, I bought the house right in front of ours for my parents. That way I could see them everyday. At ten o'clock every night, I took them for ice cream. I did this come hell or high water. When I was recording with Shakira, when the time came I'd say, "No, we have to stop," and I'd go pick up my parents.

When my mother died I had only one regret. When the family was united here in America I had spent time with my parents every day. I knew that when the fateful day arrived, as it does for all of us, there wouldn't be anything left unsaid between us, any bad feelings or any of the resentment that can stand between a grown-up child and his parents at the end of their lives. We had loved one another fully, and I feel that I honored them as much as I do my own family today. No, the only regret I have is that my mother spent years in Cuba living without freedom.

Live your family life without regret. As you build your life and business, keep in mind that it is easier to do it with the support of the ones you love. And it would be meaningless not to have them there to share in the burdens and the successes of your life.

Carmen and Emilio Estefan Sr. on their wedding day /
Carmen y Emilio Estefan en el dia de su boda

Emilio Estefan Jr.

Emilio Estefan Jr.

Carmen Gomez (grandmother), Emilio, Jose "Papo," and Antonio
Gomez (grandfather) / Carmen Gomez (abuela), Emilio, Jose "Papo," y
Antonio Gomez (abuelo)

Emilio Estefan Jr.'s passport pic-
ture when leaving Cuba for Spain /
El foto del pasaporte de Emilio
Estefan cuando viajaba de Cuba a
España

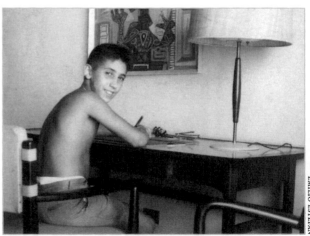

Emilio Estefan Jr. studying hard /
Emilio Estefan estudiando mucho

Emilio playing in the Capetillo Orchestra in Cuba / Emilio tocando en la orquesta Capetillo en Cuba

Emilio Estefan playing accordion with his mom, Carmen / Emilio Estefan tocando acordeón con su madre, Carmen

Emilio Estefan Jr. at WLTV Channel 23 playing on a Sunday show / Emilio Estefan en WLTV Canal 23 tocando en el show del domingo

Julia (grandmother) and Emilio / Julia (abuela) y Emilio

Aunt Javivi and Emilio / Tía Javivi y Emilio

Mr. and Mrs. Emilio Estefan on their wedding day /
El Señor y la Señora Estefan en el día de su boda

Gloria and Emilio Estefan / Gloria y Emilio Estefan

Gloria, Carmen, Emilio, Nayib, and Emilio Estefan Sr. celebrating his
parents' 50th wedding anniversary / Gloria, Carmen, Emilio, Nayib, y
Emilio Estefan, padre, celebrando el aniversario de los 50 años
de matrimonio de sus padres

Emilio and his "second mother," Gloria
Fajardo / Emilio y su "segunda madre,"
Gloria Fajardo

Emilio and his brother, Jose
"Papo" Estefan / Emilio y
su hermano, Jose
"Papo" Estefan

Emilio and Nayib with their dalmatian puppies / Emilio y Nayib con sus cachorros dálmatas

Emilio, Gloria, and Emily Estefan in Vero Beach / Emilio, Gloria, y Emily Estefan en Vero Beach

Bongos Cuban Cafe opening in Orlando / La abertura de Bongos Cuban Cafe en Orlando

Emilio and Gloria Estefan at the naming of Miami Sound Machine Blvd. / Emilio y Gloria Estefan en la inauguración del Miami Sound Machine Blvd.

Emilio Estefan, Gloria Estefan, and Marco Avila at Miami Sound Machine Platinum Record presentation / Emilio Estefan, Gloria Estefan, y Marco Avila en la presentación de un disco de platino a Miami Sound Machine

CHAPTER EIGHT

Be Yourself

H ere's a tough one: Be yourself. Sounds easy? Well, how come so many folks deviate from that? Whatever you do and however you do it, will reflect on you. It will also reveal the real you to others, and, most important, to yourself.

Reputation is the outward sign of who you are. It is your "branding," if you will. And it has to be real. It has to be authentic. It has to be you.

In business and in life a bad reputation is very easy to acquire and very difficult to shake off. Take work, for instance. When you're starting out in the working world, you begin with a clean slate. You may have submitted a résumé to secure your position, but as soon as you show up to the office or the restaurant or the building site for your first day of work, you're under the spotlight yourself. Your boss didn't hire a résumé; he or she hired a person. It's up to you. Don't blow it.

I have a lot to say through the course of this book about first impressions. When I got into the position of being the boss, I worked hard to make sure that my businesses—that is, the employees working with the customers on the front line—made a great first impression. A key person in any larger business is the person staffing the reception area. He or she is the first impression your company presents to the world. If they're friendly, helpful and efficient, great. If they won't look you in the eye or they're talking on the cell phone when a customer is trying to get attention, that's not great.

But when you're starting out, or when you are taking a new job or moving to a new country, as I did twice, it's all down to you. The best piece of advice I can give you is very simple.

Be yourself.

Okay, that's cool but what does it mean? In order to be yourself you have to know who you are: You have to know the story of your own life. I suggest you do this by first telling a friend or one of your children your life story. Sometimes other people ask us questions about ourselves and our lives that we have never thought about. A different perspective is always important. Another way of doing this is writing down the story of your life and those of your immediate family. As you can tell, if you have read this far, for me, the process of writing about the way I do business involves telling my life story.

Younger people may very reasonably say they are in the process of finding out who they are. "Ask me in a couple of years." Another way of saying "be yourself" is, "be authentic." Don't try to be someone you're not. A significant part of what constitutes *you* is your value system. So perform a values check on yourself.

You can do this at the same time that you're finding out what motivates you. What qualities do you consider most important in yourself and the people closest to you? There are certain values that will propel you forward and make you a happy, self-respecting person, someone people want to know and work with. Showing commitment, loyalty, and respect can take you a long way. These values need to be demonstrated over a long period before your name will be attached to them. But you can be proud of yourself from day one.

It's vital that you take pride in who you are. This is another reason you should know where you come from and who your parents are. That may involve finding out about who they were before they were your parents. (I know that a lot of young people can't imagine their parents as young people, but they were once!) And take pride in whatever you accomplish.

For an immigrant, pride is extremely important. As we already discussed, I took advantage of my heritage and made sure it was part of everything I accomplished moving forward in this country. It doesn't matter if you're two, five, or eight generations removed from immigration, it's still a key part of you. The further back you go in search of you, you might find some surprises. Great-great-great-great-grandpa was from where?

As you look at yourself, discovering your real motivation, finding out something about your life story, and reviewing your values, an interesting picture will develop. Coming into focus is something—you! You will see who you are. How you got here is important to understand, because you can't change what is intrinsically you, nor should you. Being who you are—being authentic, in other words—is your greatest strength. Remember who you are and how you got to be that way.

Be yourself. It sounds so simple but it covers so much. Being who you really are will determine the people you surround yourself with and the people who are attracted to you and who want to spend time with you. Being who you are will also determine what you do with your life. It will determine how you behave and how you protect your good name. And a key part of protecting your good name is to live within your means. It's a mantra: Be yourself, protect your good name, and live within your means. It's not very rock 'n' roll but it's great advice, trust me.

My entire career is based on who I am and where I come from. I have never had to compromise and pretend to be something or someone I am not. My music is really and truly *my* music and not a pale imitation of someone else's. My ideas are my own. My likes and dislikes aren't fads of the latest trendy thing. They come from me. Being authentic is the only honest way to be.

Your personality is also unique, and being yourself is first and foremost accepting who you are as a person. Once you know and accept strengths and weaknesses, it makes it easier for you to know and understand your limitations. Knowing your limitations frees you up to focus on your strengths.

One thing I have never hidden or denied to myself is that I have attention deficit disorder, ADD for short. I make no apologies, because I consider it more of an advantage than a disadvantage—and one I have learned a great deal from. My mind often races, I am very energetic, and I really hate to sit still. I knew all those things about myself long before I ever heard the term ADD. Not only have I learned to live with it; I have turned this into a gift, I believe. On the one hand, it forced me at a young age to get into the habit of being very organized—otherwise, I would never get anything done, because I would spend all my time looking for things! Another thing it taught me early on was the importance of completing things. Many with ADD have trouble completing tasks simply because they can't stay focused long enough to follow through on things, sometimes even simple tasks.

I deal with it by doing many things at once. If I am doing something that requires me to think, like ruminate on a business plan or prepare myself for a meeting or an interview, I often do it while I have a physical task that needs to be taken care of, like washing the car or doing some gardening (yes, I do both those things!).

Being yourself also means not pretending to be either less or more than you are. If you are proud of your achievements then you'll be comfortable telling people about them. In the appropriate setting, of course—no one likes a show-off. But pumping yourself up falsely can be really costly. It can cost you opportunities and it can lead you down the wrong path. Trying to be something or someone you're not is expensive.

How often do we hear of people getting in over their heads financially because they go into debt trying to appear to be more than they really are? I have been lucky in that I never had to take out very big loans in order to move forward. I was usually able to do things with my own money. I don't owe money. All that I have personally is paid for. I know not everyone can do that. In fact, it is pretty unusual. And acquiring a certain amount of debt to build up a credit history is a good thing to do.

The credit crunch that began in 2008 and the resulting recession have changed a lot of people's attitude to money. Part of the reason we got in such a mess was people taking advantage of easy credit—to a di-

sastrous extent. Borrowing money is harder to do these days, so it's easier to follow this advice: Don't spend money you don't have in order to
become someone you aren't. The root of this principle lies in your sense
of yourself. Be yourself, be proud of yourself, and always protect your
good name. You are your own good name, and your attitude toward
money comes from your sense of yourself.

How we treat money says a lot about our values and ourselves. If you
really know who you are, you will keep your spending and credit in
check. When you are starting a business or trying to grow one you'll
need financing and other types of backing. Just don't get in over your
head. How many times have you received an envelope that says, *You've
been preapproved*, and inside there is a credit card application partly
filled out with a rate and little bonuses that look so tempting. Remember: Credit cards are not cash; they are debt, and expensive debt at that.
It is a good idea to incur debt only when it's absolutely necessary to take
an important step forward, not to dig yourself into a hole you'll have a
hard time getting out of. It's easy digging too; a few unnecessary charges
each month quickly add up. Paying off that balance is like losing
weight—it's a damn sight easier going the wrong direction than it is
coming back.

For really big steps you usually do have to get loans, but you have to
be aware of what you are doing, and what your obligations are to the
person or institution lending you the money. So many immigrants (and
of course this isn't just directed at immigrants!) have taken out loans
with stringent conditions and very high interest rates. It's really hard to
get yourself out from underneath when you get into that kind of situation. Is it worth it? Probably not. Again, nothing is worth the sacrifice of
your good name.

Our relationship with money reveals an awful lot about who we are.

Treating money well is part of the good habit of being yourself. Taking out loans can be a good thing if you are educated about the process.
Get advice. I say this over and over. Get the best advice you can afford.
Borrowing money is a big deal because you have to pay it back. If you
don't do so in a timely fashion it becomes very costly and could even cost

you your good name if you default on a loan. Find out what the best terms are and what you are eligible for, and get what you need and can pay back, not more. Review your choices. If you aren't eligible for something you think you need, be patient.

Much of what I learned when I lived in Spain with my father was about living frugally. There are two sides to each coin you're spending when you're trying to live within your means: Don't borrow money you don't need and don't waste whatever money you might have.

I was talking to my son recently and he wanted to buy a house. We got into a discussion of budgeting and planning and the need to learn to do both. I said, "Listen. It would be easy for me to write a check for you right now. I don't need to spend four days fighting with you to tell you: You need to do a budget. You need to be able to support yourself. You're going to get married; you're going to have kids. With what you make right now, you can't afford a house." I'm trying to teach him what I feel it's important for him to know. It's that ancient parental advice that has every kid rolling their eyes. Money doesn't grow on trees.

My son has never had to live without, and for that I'm so grateful. Neither of my kids has ever had to go through what I had to go through. But that means they missed a lot of life lessons that I learned. Despite the tough times, I learned an awful lot about kindness—kindness and living without. It's amazing how you redefine the word "need" when you have so little. It's also interesting how you define "generosity"—it isn't how much you have and give; it's really about how little you have and how much you give of that.

My grandmother Carmen had a sister in Galicia. She knew my father and I had arrived in Spain and she helped us out as much as she could. Every so often a package would arrive from her in the mail—a box full of chorizo, perhaps, or some cheese and other foods. That felt like abundance to us, because there were many days when my father and I, probably especially my father, felt hunger pangs. We could never afford to go visit my great-aunt, and she could not afford to come to visit us. It was only years later that I learned what sacrifices she had made in order to send us that food. Gloria and I went to visit her not long after we had married. She lived very simply and was actually quite poor herself, but that didn't stop her from sharing what little she had. Those packages were often lifesavers for us. It was a kindness I will never forget.

It is humbling to think about my great-aunt and her simplicity. It puts a lot into perspective. It reminds me where I came from. It is a powerful reminder of who I am.

CHAPTER NINE

Get an Education and Keep Developing Your Skills and Talents

U nless you're going to work for yourself from day one, you're going to have to find a job. The first thing most employers look for in a job applicant is his or her education. If you leave school without any qualifications it's going to be hard to find a decent job—or any job in a tough economic climate. You may think it's a waste of time spending two extra years in school or four years in college. What you learn may not be any use in the outside world. But you might find yourself starting so many rungs down the job ladder you'll spend more time catching up than you would have staying in school or college. In most cases, you'll never catch up.

I'm not the best role model when it comes to education. Formal education and certificates weren't a priority when putting food on the table was in question. Certainly when I hire someone I look at the person rather than the piece of paper. I've hired people who don't have the right qualifications plenty of times. But everyone's not like me. And education doesn't stop with school and college.

When I was a kid in Cuba, the idea of starting school was neither particularly exciting nor particularly traumatic for me. I just wasn't very interested. Eventually the day came, and together with the other kids of my age in Santiago, I began school. What I remember most are the repeated warnings about watching what I said outside the house. At home,

I was never really scolded or punished. If anything I was indulged, especially by the women in my life, my mother and my grandmothers. So it felt strange to be spoken to so sternly by my parents and grandparents. Looking back, I realize it was just part of that general climate of fear that was beginning to permeate our life.

I didn't like school very much but I always managed to get good grades. I wasn't very keen on sitting still or being told what to do and I found it boring to follow the school schedule. Nowadays, a kid like me might be diagnosed with ADD, as my son later was. Back then, we were just dubbed "unruly" or "bored." During my school days in Cuba, I was mostly bored.

My father and his "university of the streets" attitude did not provide the greatest role model as far as completing my formal education was concerned. As I mentioned, I do agree with him to some extent: You can learn a great deal from living life outside the classroom. But my experiences when my father and I arrived in Miami serve as a reminder that you shouldn't neglect your education even if you have to work.

We stayed in a small house suitable for about four people, maybe six at the most. My uncle and aunt rented it from a very nice Polish couple who I can't imagine knew how many people were actually living there. There were often recently arrived cousins, uncles and aunts, friends: anyone who needed a place to stay while he or she or they got on their feet, got a job, and found more permanent accommodations. You stayed just as long as you needed to and moved on to make a place for the next person.

We all understood that our role—or, more important, our duty— was to lend a hand to other recent arrivals and people in need. That's how we paid back the people who had helped us. I know this story has played itself out over and over in immigrant communities all around the world. In the case of the Cuban community, the immigrant experience was especially dramatic, because it took place over the course of a few short years. That, I believe, is one of things that has made the community so strong.

I was especially happy to be with my aunt Javivi. She was a lot like my mother—simple, easygoing, and focused on the family. It was nice to feel that warmth and affection from someone with strong maternal instincts. How nice it was to get back home at the end of the day and get a hug and kiss and have my aunt ask, "How was your day? What did you do today?" I felt so grateful to have a place to stay that was more than a room; it was a home.

My hernia was bothering me a lot by the time I arrived in Miami, and I finally agreed to have the surgery. It was just getting too painful. My aunt brought me to the Variety Children's Hospital in Miami one morning at around five o'clock. She couldn't stay with me, because she had to go to the factory where she worked. She kissed me good-bye and left. I wasn't going to run out this time.

I don't remember the actual surgery, of course, because I was knocked out, but I do remember very clearly waking up in a lot of pain and not being able to communicate anything about it because I spoke so little English. I'm a strong person, but that experience freaked me out. My throat was completely parched. I was able to call out, "Water," but not much else. I was very relieved when my aunt came to see me after work.

Although I was happy to be in Miami—a place that was much more similar than Madrid to Cuba, with its warm weather, palm trees, and the ocean—there were rough times. As I had in Spain, I also went hungry some nights. Still, I felt optimistic, so I immediately set about finding ways to make money.

I remembered the conversation I had with my brother the night before I left Havana. Repeatedly in his letters to me in Spain he'd tell me how important it was to get a good education, or to at least finish school. I confess that was not as high on my list of priorities as finding work. Making money meant I'd be closer to being able to bring my family to the United States—or at least, that was how I saw it right then.

I did realize that we needed to have as solid a foundation to our lives as possible in the United States, and a formal education would help greatly. The key thing that made me pursue my studies was that I knew that going to school would help me learn English. I was pretty much surrounded by Cubans in my day-to-day life, and it probably would have been easy enough to just live in Spanish. But I knew that wouldn't get me very far in the long run. Back then, in the late sixties, Miami was still overwhelmingly a city in the southern United States and not the "Gateway to the Americas" that it has become. Despite the huge influx of Cubans in a period of a few short years, English still ruled and Spanish was not widely spoken. To get ahead, you needed to speak English. And I believe that should absolutely be a priority for all immigrants today. You need to take it upon yourself to learn English. It is still vital to getting ahead here.

I registered for high school and started immediately. I didn't have any part-time work, or even any very good prospects for a job, until one day a friend of the family we'd known back in Santiago told me about an opening at Bacardi, the liquor company where he worked. Of course, I was very familiar with the company—you couldn't be from Santiago in Cuba and not know about Bacardi or the famous family who'd founded it. And remember, my grandmother Carmen had gone to work for Bacardi when she arrived in Cuba from Spain, and my grandfather had asked Don Emilio Bacardi, head of the family and son of the founder, Facundo, for permission to marry her. I also had personal links—both my brother and I had been to school with Bacardis in Santiago. These connections made it seem like a happy coincidence.

Our friend told me about the job, and he said I'd have to lie about my age because you had to be eighteen to work there. The guy who was recruiting took one look at me and said, "You're not eighteen," and I said, "Yes, you're right, I'm not. I'm fifteen and a half, but I need to work." The man said he wanted to help me, but the only way he could hire me was for me to be in school, so I got a permit to attend school at night at Lindsey Hopkins Tech in downtown Miami.

I really wanted that job badly, so I was thrilled when I got hired to work in the mailroom. My English was terrible—someone would say, "Go to the third floor," and I didn't know what the hell they were telling me. The people were so nice to me, wanting to help, so we figured out a system where basic instructions—"*Segundo piso* is second floor"—were written on pieces of paper. The job was Monday to Friday, and I went to night school from four to eight p.m. right after I finished work, five days a week.

Bacardi is one of the fixtures in my life. The company and the family were each a big presence in my hometown, so I was always aware of them. Then I got my first job in America working at Bacardi and I stayed there for years. It's another way I can measure how far I've come. I started my working life as a non-English-speaking office boy at Bacardi, and now my restaurants sell more Bacardi rum than any other establishments in Florida.

It was exciting to get my first paycheck. It wasn't a lot of money, but it felt like a great beginning. I saved as much as I possibly could, spending only what was absolutely necessary to get by. There were times when I barely had enough money to buy food because I was so intent on saving. I got very good at doing without. Sometimes on my way home from work, I'd stop at a store and buy a bottle of milk and a couple of day-old doughnuts, and that would be my dinner. (It's amazing how nostalgic you can get about hard times: To this day, I still prefer stale doughnuts.)

At around the same time I started working for Bacardi, I started to do odd jobs around the neighborhood on weekends to earn extra money. Before long, I'd saved enough money to buy a beat-up old Volkswagen Bug. It got me around, and having wheels helped me find more work. I didn't always get paid with money; a lot of times I accepted barter—a run to the grocery store or picking someone up in exchange for an iron and an ironing board, or I would help someone move and in return they would give me a vacuum cleaner, a couple of dishes. I accepted goods in exchange for my services because I wanted to furnish an apartment or a house for when my family would get to Miami. I was motivated by getting a home ready for my mother.

About six months after I arrived in Florida, my father was able to join me. I had petitioned for him as soon as I got to the United States, and my aunt and uncle started to save for his flight as well. I hoped that from then on, I'd be able to pay to get my family out of Cuba and to Miami. My father and I stayed on with my aunt for a while until we had saved enough to move out to an apartment of our own.

Despite making work a priority, I understood I'd be much better off in the long run if I could speak English and finish high school in the American system. So I did both—I worked and went to school. It's vitally important: Never stop educating yourself. Education is important, but formal education is not the only way to go. Formal education does have its limitations in the practical world. You can have all kinds of degrees, but if you don't know how to listen and to give straight answers, you aren't going to impress too many people for too long. (And I can't tell you how many educated people I have met over the years who have no street savvy or little common sense!)

The path of learning should extend into the workplace. I was already working when I was in high school, and I continued to work throughout college. You can learn an awful lot at work, especially if you start young. You can learn organization, planning, and how to deal with a broad cross section of people, all important skills that you are going to need over and over in business—and in life!

Getting a formal education is an essential part of a well-thought-out plan. You should try to get formal schooling not necessarily to become an expert in any particular area. It's more important because it forces you to be disciplined and it helps you learn how to learn. You're faced with subject matter you're not familiar with, and you need to know how to acquaint yourself with it without panicking. Studying gives you a sense of accomplishment, it can help provide security to you and your family, and it shows people who deal with you in business that you are capable of completing something challenging.

If you put together what you know intuitively with what you learn on the street, at work, and in life, together with your formal education, you've created a winning combination. If you're dealing with numbers but don't have an accounting background, you use your formal education to learn how to read and understand those numbers. You also use your savvy and your intuition to know when something looks good or not. When you use all the forms of learning at your disposal, then you're well-placed to take advantage.

CHAPTER TEN

Do What You Love to Do

I am extremely grateful that I discovered I had a talent for music. You should take stock of your personal assets. If you have a special talent, develop it and nurture it. I have loved music for as long as I can remember, and it has never been a problem for me to practice an instrument every day. If you love something, you almost can't help doing it. And when I realized in my teens that I liked doing business and had a talent for that too, I almost never missed a chance to try to develop a business or to negotiate a deal.

If you want to account for where I am today, it all started with an accordion.

One day when I was seventeen, I walked past a music store in downtown Miami and there it was in the window: an accordion, its white keys glistening in the afternoon sun. Something was missing from my life: making music. I had been playing since I was seven years old, but I hadn't played in a while, mainly because I hadn't owned an accordion since I had left Cuba several years before. In Spain, I had played in a restaurant with a borrowed accordion, but I'd never really gotten the opportunity to practice or play with other musicians just for fun.

I wanted that accordion. I wanted it so badly I could almost feel it in my hands. In my mind, I could already hear the music I wanted to make.

My father and I were still living with my uncle and aunt at the time, and I ran home and found my uncle and started pleading with him: "*Tío*, come with me. I need your help." As we made our way back to the store, I explained that I needed him to cosign a loan so that I could buy that accordion. I made my case to my uncle. I knew that was a way I could make money. I said I should be able to pay off the loan in a relatively short time. It wasn't hard for me to convince him to do it. After all, he had been a successful businessman and knew that making money often involved some risk. It certainly involved sacrifice and investment.

We got to the store and I held the accordion. The feel of the instrument in my hands was so familiar to me, and I hugged the accordion close to me. My uncle and I left a small down payment and signed the papers. Then the store owner put the accordion in its case and handed it over. It was mine.

Later, we arrived home with the accordion and a debt of $277. My aunt hit the roof: "What were you two thinking?" I want to tell you just what I was thinking and what I told my aunt that day. It is as true today as it was almost forty years ago, and it is at the very core of my philosophy of happiness in life and work.

"I need to do something I love," was what I said.

The feeling was overpowering, so overpowering that I was willing to persuade my uncle to cosign for money he didn't have to allow me to play music again. Music was healing for me. I wanted to make music. And I needed to make money. Music was a way to fulfill myself, and I also saw it as a way to supplement my earnings. As it turns out, I was right on both counts. The purchase of that accordion set off a chain of events that has led up to my life till now.

I loved music from a very early age, listening to it and making it. Music was the one thing that I could concentrate on easily as a kid, and which kept my attention for long periods of time. My family wasn't particularly musical, but you cannot be Cuban—especially from Santiago— and not love music. The city is famed for its musical traditions, and it is the cradle of many of Cuba's unique styles. We were surrounded by music, and it was as much a part of our daily lives in Santiago as the warm breeze that blew off the Caribbean. Of Santiago, I remember the mountains and the sea, and I remember the music.

Every year in July, there was a big carnival in Santiago. The musicians and other participants would dress up in wild, colorful costumes and dance to the never-ending music. There would be enormous conga lines of thousands of people. I loved seeing people having so much fun, but I especially loved the music.

What I remember best were the rhythms; they were so contagious, and they stuck in your head. Many musical styles were born in Santiago; they were usually the fusion of African rhythms brought over by slaves centuries before, with sounds that originated in Europe. The genres most commonly associated with Santiago and eastern Cuba are *trova* and *son*. *Trova* is music made by wandering groups of musicians, something like the troubadours of Europe, and there is a festival every year in Santiago of that type of music. People gather in parks and plazas all over the city (as well as more formal venues) and make music.

Son is possibly associated even more closely with Santiago and is the perfect example of an Afro-Cuban genre. *Son* has a distinctive rhythm that is driven by the bass line, and it is heavily percussive. Playing *son*, musicians typically use claves (polished pieces of hardwood that are struck together with a rhythm) and conga and bata drums (both of which are African in origin). Our city was home to famous musicians, like Compay Segundo (of *Buena Vista Social Club*) and Desi Arnaz (before he was Lucy's husband, he was a famous bandleader in the United States).

I can't remember when I first heard music, but I do remember when I started making it. I was about seven years old when I got my first accordion. It was a gift for *Día de los Reyes*—the Day of the Kings. In Cuba we don't celebrate Christmas Day with presents. We receive gifts on January 6, the feast of Epiphany, which is the day the three kings brought presents to the baby Jesus. I remember being very pleased and excited about having my own musical instrument, even if it was just a toy. Soon I was playing the accordion for hours by myself. Come to think of it, maybe that's why I was given the instrument. My mom probably needed me out of her hair, and it seemed like a good way to keep me occupied.

It turned out that I had a talent for the accordion. Before I knew it, I was picking out songs: "La Chambelona," "Siboney," "Quiéreme Mucho" were among the first. I could hear a tune and play it on the accordion. Soon I was playing at family gatherings. And fortunately for me there were a lot of these get-togethers—they gave me lots of opportunity to practice and to fine-tune my playing and performing skills.

A FEW OF THE GUYS in the neighborhood—Agustincito, Pundi, Carlitos, Danielito—also loved music. We started hanging out together, and instead of just the usual boyish pursuits, playing ball or war games or cops and robbers, we started making music together. Apart from my toy accordion and a toy guitar, we didn't have much in the way of instruments, so we used a couple of sticks, spoons, pots and pans—whatever we could get our hands on. We had enough stuff to make our own fun, and we actually started to get pretty good!

One magical day, my father returned from a trip to Havana laden with gifts. He had won big at a poker game there (or he may have won the lottery again), and because he was so generous he always brought back presents not just for the family and extended family, but often for friends as well. This time he brought back instruments, real musical instruments. He brought guitars, bongos, *tumbadoras* (a type of conga drum), claves, and, most special of all—an accordion, a real accordion!

Everyone was thrilled, especially me. My father couldn't have given me a better gift if he had asked me what I wanted out of everything in the world. To this day, that accordion is the most thoughtful and appreciated gift I have ever received. The guys and I considered ourselves "real" musicians, and we took our vocation seriously. We gave our group a name: El Conjunto Capetillo, in honor of my father. We practiced a lot and got so good that we were able to play for tips at parties. Within a year of starting the group, we were hired to play at clubs and carnivals, and once we made about $75—a fortune! And then we appeared on a national TV program.

Not long after that trip to Havana, my father had to stop playing poker. The Communist government had outlawed gambling, and it was too dangerous for my father to continue in that line of business. Making music and playing with El Conjunto Capetillo constituted an oasis in my life in Cuba for me. And I kept playing until the day I left the country.

When my father and I left the country I wasn't able to take my accordion with me, and music left my life for the first time I could remember. Until one day in Madrid, I found a restaurant that let me play music for its patrons in exchange for meals for my father and me. I borrowed the accordion of the musician who played in the restaurant weekday evenings. I played in the off-peak hours.

Music, which had long been my solace and my escape, became one of my means of survival. Soon people started paying me for requests, and I also received tips. That money was very helpful. I learned that every little bit helps. And making music again was helping to heal my soul. It kept me focused and reminded me that all this suffering and this loneliness I was suffering were for a bigger purpose.

Moving forward to Miami, once I had my precious accordion, I played again, practicing every spare minute I had (which wasn't many). I saved and saved and began to make payments on the loan we'd taken out to buy the instrument. I felt a lot of pride every time I made a payment, in monthly installments of $17.58. I knew at the time, and I know it still today: You can pay off a debt, but you can't pay off a regret. Sometimes you have to invest in what you love and take a chance.

I wanted to branch out and play more instruments, and I wanted to play with other musicians. I couldn't afford to buy anything else at that point, what with living expenses, and saving to bring my family from Cuba. But one day I hit upon an idea that I figured might be worth trying. I had been eyeing a guitar in a music store, knowing I couldn't afford it but wishing so very much that I could. I approached the store owner and offered a barter deal: In exchange for the guitar, I would work Saturday afternoons at the store, cleaning the accordions he rented and sold, and tuning the guitars. To my delight, the owner agreed to my proposal.

I started to play accordion along with two violinists, first for tips, in an Italian restaurant on Miami's Biscayne Boulevard, on nights and weekends after school and after my day job working in the mailroom at Bacardi. I'd go to school, change in the car, and go to the restaurant to play accordion. A coworker at Bacardi soon asked me to join him in a band. We played our first gig at an office party and everything snowballed from there: birthdays, first communions, bar mitzvahs, *quinces*—you name it, we played it. And I was doing what I loved to do.

I won't say that juggling my work schedule and my studies was easy, but I was highly motivated—in part out of necessity—but what kept me going was that I loved what I was doing. That's absolutely fundamental to my success. I found something I loved to do and found a way to make a living doing it.

Is it that easy? Yes. Okay, no—but almost. Knowing what you love is almost half the battle. So if you don't already know what you love, figuring that out is the first step. Don't delude yourself by thinking something will bring you fame and fortune (or at least fortune) and that you will fall in love with it later. And just because something's a worthy and noble profession doesn't mean you'll love it. (Though I've always believed music is an uplifting profession because it brings joy to the person making it and to the person enjoying it.)

You may have to try your hand at a number of different things before you find what you love, but be persistent. You should soon figure out your calling.

Why is it so important to do what you love? Part of the answer is obvious: You will grow tired of something you aren't completely committed to, you'll become frustrated, and eventually you'll probably start going through the motions. A big part of living your dream is enjoying yourself along the way. It's so important to enjoy life as much as you can. If you can achieve success doing something you love, there is nothing better.

CHAPTER ELEVEN

Develop a Plan

Y ou're motivated and you've taken responsibility for your own actions. If you're lucky you've found something you love to do. You're committed to improving your prospects with education or training. You're keeping that positive outlook on life. The next step is to develop a plan and then to keep planning over and over. I had a plan that day when I saw and bought the accordion. Maybe I hadn't articulated what the plan was too clearly, even to myself, but there was more behind that purchase than just wanting to horse around, and I knew that instinctively.

The larger purpose was already in place, with the desire to reunite my whole family in the freedom of the United States, but I had not developed a proper plan to make that happen. The fact that I could do something I loved was a bonus. Of course, I was also motivated by the need—and the desire!—to pay off the accordion—my first debt—but that is a smaller part of the story. . . .

I formulated the plan as soon as I got the accordion home from the store. I continued to work all day at Bacardi, and after night school I headed off to make music. I was a young man with a plan! The pieces of a plan had fallen into place, and within a couple of years it bore some wonderful fruit.

I had a great run at Bacardi. It was then, and it is now, a great company to work for. It nurtures its employees, and I always felt I had plenty of opportunity there—to learn and to grow. But at some point I was going to want to do something for myself, something that I could really run and call my own. I remember having that longing not because I disliked Bacardi—for the opposite reason, in fact. The company was a great teacher. It was my business school, for all practical purposes. I saw how well Bacardi managed employees, and of course I experienced that myself firsthand. My work was recognized and rewarded, and I felt appreciated and that what I did day in and day out was important.

I did everything at Bacardi. I was always positive and I made myself available. "I need to work. What do you want me to do?" I said I'd work weekends for extra money. I'd go to bars for promotions, whatever they wanted. Other people are always much more willing to help someone with that kind of attitude than a lazy, work-shy person. It just makes sense.

It wasn't long before I moved from the mailroom into the marketing department. I enjoyed that immensely. I became assistant to a guy called Andy Fernandez who'd gone to school with my brother. He wanted to help me. I realized—as did my employers—that I had a knack for marketing. What are marketers? The short definition is that they are promoters of an idea, a concept. They are resourceful in that they have to be able to translate something tangible into something abstract (or sometimes vice versa). For instance, how often have you seen a soft drink, an article of clothing, or another product defined as part of a lifestyle? Often, a product will be barely mentioned in a campaign. What is played up is how a product adds to the consumer's life. You have to be pretty clever to make that leap. And it's a lot of fun to do.

Another terrific aspect of working at Bacardi was their openness to ideas. It didn't matter who you were or where you worked in the company; if you had an idea, someone would listen. If it was a good idea, there was usually someone willing to take a chance on it and help you to execute it.

When I started working in the marketing department at Bacardi, I had an idea for a business venture within the company. I hadn't been working there for long, but I could already see that Bacardi had a very creative way to push its brands beyond doing ads. They held contests, they had tastings, they sponsored festivals, and they made T-shirts. One day while I was placing an order for T-shirts, I realized I could actually have them made myself, and cheaper. I used decals on the shirt instead of painting. I showed Bacardi the sample and they liked the shirt. I went to the T-shirt company with the purchase order and the guy said, "I'll do it for you," and that was the first big money I made. Bacardi saved money, I made a buck on each T-shirt, and everyone was happy.

The other great thing about Bacardi's corporate culture was that its managers took an interest in their employees and their lives. It was no secret that I loved music—I talked about music a lot. Many of the people I worked with were also Cuban, and we all missed home and our culture, so music was a common bond and a topic of conversation.

Tito Argamasilla Bacardi, one of the directors of Bacardi, knew I was a musician and that I moonlighted at a restaurant. His family had a big birthday party coming up, and Tito was in charge of entertainment. He asked me if I could come to the party and play the accordion, just for a couple of hours. I saw this as a great opportunity. This could potentially be a high-profile engagement for me, and I decided to take the risk of not making any money myself on the gig, and I hired a guitarist and a percussionist for that evening. I was excited to get the chance to play with other musicians as well.

I offered to play at the party and to do it for tips. I arranged to come with a couple of other musicians. The whole family was there, and I was given a nice tip at the end of the evening.

The evening of the party turned into a very special one for me. We had been hired to play till about ten thirty, but we wound up staying till four o'clock in the morning, stopping for only a few short breaks. Call it nostalgia or a good vibe, whatever, but the guests were enjoying themselves so much that they kept making requests, and we just kept on playing. The band was having as good a time as the guests. I knew all the old Cuban songs and I played them all. That seemed to feed a need at the party. The guests identified so much with the music that they didn't want it to stop. And neither did I.

We did well that night. We earned a lot in tips, and most important of all, we got the most fantastic exposure. We played the music we loved for people who loved that type of music. We had found our audience and they had found us. From that night, things snowballed. The same group of guys started to play every weekend, as often as two or three times a weekend. And the Miami Latin Boys were born.

My hunch about the accordion was paying off.

I was thinking all the time about my family back in Cuba: my mother, brother, sister-in-law, niece, and my little baby nephew. As well as I was doing, my existence was fairly meaningless without them with me. Staying in touch was very difficult. Back then, it would take nothing short of a miracle to get a telephone call through. It could take hours to make a connection, and the operator would tell you that she would call back as soon as she got through. And even then, you often didn't get through.

Because any kind of communication was so infrequent, it was rare to get information about the family. Sometimes we would hear news through recent arrivals, new families from Santiago, but relatively few people had visited Santiago recently enough for them to have any fresh news. Getting my family back together continued to be the driving force behind all my hard work, even if at times it felt like it might still be years before we could get them out.

I was saving as much money as I possibly could to pay for my family to be able to travel. There were still no direct flights between Cuba and the United States, so when my family would come, they would have to go via a third country, like Spain, as my father and I did. That would make it all the more expensive. I was very aware of that, but never discouraged by it.

I managed to save about $1,200, and I tucked it away in a safe place. My father knew about the money, and at that point my money was certainly "our" money. One day I came home and found the money was gone, and my father with it. He was gone for the next two days. I didn't worry, either about him or the money, because I realized that he had taken it in order to play in a poker game. Since more often than not he won, I didn't think too much about the money or the hard work it had taken to save it. But the longer he was gone, the more I began to doubt I would see the money again. And sure enough, that was what happened. My father had taken the money for a game, but this time he lost it—every penny of it.

That was disappointing, to say the least. But I knew my father, and it wasn't surprising. It wasn't the first time he had been absolutely irresponsible about money, and it wouldn't be the last. I couldn't get mad at him. I knew him too well, and really, I simply loved him too much. I had earned that money before; I would earn it again. That kind of setback wasn't enough to derail me.

I had faith that my long-term plan was going to work. I was learning so much at Bacardi and taking advantage of the opportunities that were presenting themselves to me there. I also created my own opportunities by letting everyone know that I was willing to work and could try my hand at anything. In the meantime my English was improving and I was working on it. But Bacardi was always a means to an end, not the end in itself. I knew that my music was going to take me farther than my job in the corporation, no matter how well I was doing there. I was constantly changing my plan and revising my sights higher and higher. One of my dreams was about to be realized.

CHAPTER TWELVE

Keep Planning

M y mother's exit visa from Cuba was finally granted in 1970. But there were still no direct flights from Cuba to the United States, so my mother bought a ticket to Mexico City, not quite knowing how she was going to get to the United States from there. At least she would be out of Cuba; even though she'd now be physically somewhat farther away, she would be much closer to us. We knew it was legally possible for Cubans to cross from Mexico to the United States. There were no diplomatic relations between the United States and Cuba at the time—neither an embassy nor consular officials. In 1977, both countries established interests sections in each other's capitals, which made getting visas a lot easier. Direct travel wasn't reestablished for a few more years.

I know very little of the details of my mother's departure from Cuba, just that, as happy as she was to be joining my father and me, she was desperately sad to leave my brother and his family behind. Her parents had both died by then. My brother insisted that my mother leave. We all saw that as the next step to bringing the family back together.

My mother arrived in Mexico City and soon made arrangements to get to Miami. She didn't have papers to enter the United States, even though it was legal for Cubans to enter and take up residence. The problem was, we didn't have the money to support her there while all the paperwork was sorted out. With a family we knew from Santiago, my mother traveled by land to the U.S.-Mexican border, and when she arrived there, she paid a coyote (a guide) to take her to the other side.

But when she got to the Rio Grande there was a problem crossing the river. In Miami we were waiting to hear from her, and we didn't hear a thing for days. We were distraught. I was so tense I was losing my mind. Had she been kidnapped? You can imagine all the thoughts that were running through my head. I finally got a call from my mom saying she was in Houston and flying into Miami that evening. She'd been hiding all that time because of border guard activity in the area.

So my mother crossed into the United States illegally, like so many before her and since. Being Cuban, as soon as you got to the United States you could change your immigration status right away with no consequence. My father and I were overjoyed. It had been the longest four years of my life.

My dream of reuniting my family was partly realized with my first plan. My whole family wasn't reunited, but my mother had been able to get out of Cuba using the proceeds of my various jobs, mostly profits from playing with the Miami Latin Boys. My love of music and my determination to capitalize on my musical talents had paid off. I kept my full-time job at Bacardi, and I was on my way to earning more money from that source too. And I got my high school diploma in the meantime, which enabled me to go on to college—night school again—to study business administration.

My first plan set me on my way. But it sure wasn't my last plan. It was just the beginning of a really good habit I developed early on. I plan and I replan, if you will, and I build on plans. And when I talk of planning, I'm certainly not just referring to planning for your business. Plan for all the goals in your life: your studies, your finances, your vacations, and especially your family.

Plans should be solid, but that doesn't mean they should be inflexible. Being solid means that you take into consideration as many elements as possible for your plan: the goal, resources, possible obstacles, or other outcomes. But plans can change along the way, and that's part of the reason you need to plan, to be able to deal with the unexpected and still continue to work toward your goals. And if you figure out a better way to get from A to B, then change the plan accordingly. You can suffer setbacks, as I did when my father took the money I had saved and blew it in a poker game, but you have to regroup and dive back in with even greater determination.

I never would have expected when I was a kid in Cuba that my life would have taken the route it has. I certainly didn't have fifty years plotted out. I had to adapt to new circumstances—some pretty dramatic new circumstances when I first left Cuba—and I have had to continually adapt along the way. But planning has allowed me to do that.

Most young people want to party and not plan and think about their old age or even their short-term future. Immigrants don't have that luxury. Either you are struggling to survive in a new country or you are scrambling to send money to your family at home. Or both. Whatever your situation, as an immigrant you know only too well how important it is to plan and to budget and to think ahead to a better future. After all, isn't that better future what we came to this country for in the first place?

I get teased a lot by those close to me for how *much* I plan to this day. I mean, I really do plan everything, beginning with my daily routine. Time is one of your most important resources and you have to use it wisely, so you need to plan your day—or schedule, in other words. It's amazing how much you can get done in a day if you calculate realistically how long things take and if you discipline yourself to follow your schedule. Sound boring? It's not. I've found that the more I respect a schedule, the more time I seem to gain.

I enjoy a full and active life, and I like to be involved in many activities in both my private and professional life. I am very dedicated to friends and family, I'm involved in activities in my daughter's school, I like sports, I like to travel and really enjoy family vacations. Professionally, I am constantly branching out into new areas, and I've been doing that since my teens.

The only way I can live my life so fully is by planning. Even down to small things, which might seem insignificant, I like to plan. When I travel, for instance, I pack my own suitcases and I prepare for various contingencies (weather and others). I travel light but I never run out of clothes, and I never misplace items when I travel because I know what I need and I pack accordingly. I have each day's clothes packed separately so they're right at hand when I need them. This habit is deeply ingrained now, I realize that, and it really has saved me so much grief over the years!

As I write this I'm staying in a hotel. Right now, if you go to my hotel you'll see I'm ready for tonight and tomorrow. I'm away for six days, and I know what I'm going to wear every day. Otherwise my suitcase is packed. I pack up my toothbrush and I can leave in two minutes. You'll hardly even know there's someone staying in the room. I always make my own bed, so it's never untidy. I hang up the clothes I need to hang, put the valuables in the safe, and everything else is in its place in the suitcase.

When I go out of the house in the morning I have my cell phone and my wallet. I put rubber bands around my wallet to hold any receipts I get. My driver's license is always at the front, facing out, so I know where it is when I'm asked to show it.

I also carry an iPod with me in my suitcase. It's got everything I could possibly need on it. It's got all my songs. You want a song from the first Miami Sound Machine album? It's right there. Something I produced for Jon Secada back in the day? Check. I also have photographs of my hotels and my house; movies I've done; TV shows I produced. So if anything ever comes up while I'm away from the office or on the road, I have the answer at hand.

You go to my car too and everything is perfect. I have a Hummer and two Smart cars, which are great for parking on the busy streets in South Beach in Miami. The Hummer I have because I like to go comfortable and I like to go safe. Is it neat? You won't find a soda cup in my car in a million years.

Look at my office. My desk doesn't have a piece of paper on it. I have a memory like an elephant. I forget nothing. I like to go early to the airport. I'm never late to an appointment. All of these kinds of small details go into a well-organized, well-planned life. It's the way I am, but it's also the way I want to be. If planning and organization don't come naturally to you the way they do to me, they can be learned. It's essential, if you are to maximize your chance of succeeding in business, to be meticulous in your planning and execution of everything you do.

Time and money really are intimately linked. A good example is studio time. Studio time is expensive, in large part because there are a lot of highly skilled and talented people involved in recording. After thirty years in the music business, I have a pretty good idea of how long it takes to record, so when I am producing I allot what I consider a reasonable amount of studio time, and I don't go over it. I expect artists to show up prepared (punctuality and preparedness are the hallmarks of the true professional, in my opinion) so as not to waste my time or theirs. The studio isn't the place to rehearse; it's the place to record.

When we first recorded the Miami Latin Boys years ago, we had to do things in one take; if we were lucky, maybe two. That taught me the importance of rehearsing and getting things right before we even went into the studio, and that is all part of planning.

Why plan? Because you get so much more out of what you do and what you have. Whatever your resources—time, money, personnel—it is good to maximize them, to be frugal with them, and to plan with them.

Make "plan, plan, plan" your mantra. And planning isn't just long-term planning. You need to plan in the short term and in the medium term too. And don't be afraid to review and revise your plans on a regular basis. So get yourself a plan and keep planning and planning. Get into the habit of planning. And don't ever lose that habit, no matter how successful you become—you want to stay successful, right?

CHAPTER THIRTEEN

Work Hard

O nce your plans are laid, get to work on them. This is a good point to step back and assess some of my business principles, all of which were established when I was setting out on my journey as a young man in Miami.

The essence of my thinking about work can be distilled into four words: Work hard; work smart. The first principle may seem obvious but it isn't. Who knows how many great plans have never been executed because someone simply hasn't followed up? Or they have gone down the road a ways but given up because the going got a little rough? You can't be afraid to work hard. "Nobody ever died of hard work," the saying goes, but that doesn't stop a lot of people from being afraid of knuckling down, does it? And don't think working smart means you're going to be able to slack off. It's about maximizing the results of your best efforts, not making shortcuts!

So, to first principles. Work hard. For a lot of people "work" is a four-letter word. Add "hard" to that, and you're really talking dirty. Maybe that's a result of our worship of the culture of leisure. There is nothing wrong with working hard. And if you want to do your own thing and realize your dreams, that is precisely what you are going to have to do.

Of course, this ties in with defining your own success, which we discussed in chapter four. Perhaps you've reached a stage of your career when you want to spend more time at home. You don't want to have to work that hard anymore. That's a goal in itself. If you can work less hard without reducing your standard of living, that's got to be working smart! I can never really see myself slacking off. I want to keep pushing forward, being creative as long as I possibly can. It's what I've done my whole working life.

Consider my experience as an immigrant. I worked my rear end off when I came to this country. Many immigrants are incredibly hardworking—one job usually isn't enough to make ends meet. I worked at Bacardi and attended high school and played my accordion in a restaurant at night all at the same time in my teenage years. It makes me tired even to think about it now, but when I was young it seemed only natural that I'd work as hard as my mind and body could stand. Even if he or she can cover their expenses with one job, an immigrant rarely feels secure enough relying on just one source of income.

While that feeling of insecurity is often painful, it's also something that challenges you to do more, to be better, to organize and plan and to respect the value of money and the resources you have. Few immigrants to the United States complain about or are afraid of hard work. That's what we came here to do—to better ourselves through the work we could do. It's always an excellent example to follow and also to set. Never be afraid to work hard.

I have always been eager to set a good example, now as much as ever. Be the first to arrive at the office, and the last to leave. If you are the boss, that kind of leadership is essential. How can you ask your employees to do what you aren't willing to do? And if you are not yet the boss, getting to the job first and leaving last—key elements in working hard and smart—are essential if you're going to become the boss one day yourself.

Whenever you arrive at work, make sure you're turning up on time. You have to be punctual. I'm almost obsessive about being on time, if for no other reason than that it's just plain rude to keep people waiting. Wasting everyone's time by being late is more than just bad manners. Time is extremely valuable, and bad timekeeping is the height of inefficiency. Those fifteen nonproductive minutes you wasted because you're kept waiting by a tardy appointment are fifteen minutes that are gone forever.

It helps to think of time as another nonrenewable resource, like oil and natural gas, and everyone knows it's a smart idea to be frugal with resources. We talk about buying time, but that is just a funny expression. No matter how rich you are, you can't do it. Use what time you have and use it well.

You should extend the good habit of being on time into all areas of your life. Don't just be on time for meetings with other people (or lunch, drinks, or dinner, for that matter), but be on time with your own goals. That means don't procrastinate. Never, ever leave something that you can do that day for another day, be it a personal matter, like a phone call to a friend to say hello, or finishing off a budget, paying your bills, or getting a quote on a new car. If something is part of your plan for that day, or even if it is something that presents itself on the spur of the moment, don't delay.

Being on time can be very difficult to achieve. If you live and work in a big city, traffic and public transportation can mean delays. You have to factor that in. If a car ride takes twenty minutes on a good day, you still have to leave thirty. It's tough to extend that thinking into all areas of your life. Do it enough and it becomes first a habit and then a way of life.

I ALWAYS SAY THAT MY employees don't work for me; they work with me. And believe me, I am there with them, *hombro a hombro* (shoulder to shoulder), literally and figuratively. Gloria and I own a restaurant in South Beach, on the famous Ocean Drive, called Larios on the Beach. We bought Larios on the Beach in 1991, and it was, along with real estate, one of our first ventures outside of music. But it had been a while since anyone had done anything to the place and it needed a face-lift. When we were renovating Larios on the Beach, I was there every day at seven a.m., along with the handymen and the contractors. I was basically the foreman on the job, and I often opened up the restaurant, and I certainly often closed it too. I carried buckets and I pounded nails into walls. Why? At that point in my career it wasn't as if I couldn't afford to hire someone else to wield a hammer or sweep up and paint.

The fact was, I couldn't hire someone to set the example as the boss. I think that meant a lot to everyone who worked on the renovation. They could see very clearly by my example, my positive energy and enthusiasm, how important their work was and what their efforts meant to me. Nothing replaces hard work, and few things are more effective at motivating people than a hardworking boss.

You have to show you're in it for the long haul by making hard work a habit. That means you're showing commitment. This is a tough one that might not come too naturally to a lot of people either. If you're the boss and you're first in and last out on Monday, you've got to be prepared to do it on Friday too. And Saturday if you have to. And if you're not yet the boss, you have to demonstrate to the boss that you're willing to do it. If you work for yourself you probably demonstrate that commitment as a matter of course. There's no one else to pick up any slack. The buck starts and stops with you, and if you weren't committed, you'd be doing something where you were less exposed.

Something else that's tied in with commitment and working hard is the notion of persistence. Essentially it means keep trying; don't give up. It's a constant in my life: Someone says no, I redouble my efforts. Don't tell me I can't.

I think of when we started pushing our distinctive Miami sound that fused American and Cuban music in a unique blend. How many people told us the sound would never catch on? Everyone. In the 1970s there wasn't the well-defined Latino market that there is today, so we had to pioneer our way into the market ourselves. It was hard to do; the challenges at time seemed insurmountable, and there was plenty of resistance. But we were certainly persistent, and in the end it paid off, as I knew it would.

I think commitment is also about follow-through, about keeping your word to yourself and to others. This quality is one that will see you through when the going gets tough. You have to embrace the idea that being committed is the right thing to do. Commitment is about doing things on time, about completing things, seeing them through to the end. It's about paying bills, and figuring out how you can pay bills and keep paying them.

Commitment is so much a part of my life that if I gave it too much thought, I might feel overwhelmed! Besides my family obligations, I run a company with over a dozen different businesses. I feel committed to each and every employee working in each one of them, and I feel strongly that I can't let the employees down. Running our company smoothly and growing it will assure the livelihoods of the people who work for the company. Taking care of the business is akin to taking care of the family.

As my career has moved along I've adjusted my horizon. First I was responsible for only myself. Then for myself and my father when we were in Spain, and soon for my parents and me in Miami. As I started my own family my plans changed, and what I thought of as success changed too, though with the basic core remaining intact. But hard work remained a constant, along with commitment and persistence and a drive that would never allow me to give up.

You don't give up out of boredom or frustration. You don't give up when one of your enterprises suffers a setback. You don't give up if something happens in your personal life. You don't give up when the economy goes sour and the future looks a little bleak. You don't give up. Ever.

CHAPTER FOURTEEN

Work Smart

T here's more to success than simply working hard. It's important to work smart—to be efficient, to get the most out of yourself and your employees. You could say that this whole book is about working smart, but we'll just lay out some of the foundations of the concept here. There are some simple habits that allow you to really get ahead in work, and if you don't already have these habits, they are good ones to develop.

We've already mentioned some above: Be punctual and don't procrastinate. When you think about what you're trying to accomplish you can see that procrastination and delay can mean you fail to take advantage of chances that present themselves to you.

Life is full of missed opportunities, and we're just as likely to miss them in our professional lives as we are in our personal lives if we get in the habit of putting things off.

Something that happened when we were renovating Larios on the Beach has stuck in my mind. On the day we were going to open the restaurant we wanted to kick off by noon, but we weren't ready, so we were forced to put off the opening until the evening. It was something beyond our control—things like this happen. But what bothered me was something spontaneous that I didn't act on.

A man came by for lunch, saying he had come over by bus because he thought the restaurant would be opened as planned. I overheard one of the waiters telling him, "Sorry, sir, but the kitchen isn't open." I was very busy at that precise moment, but how I wish I had dropped what I was doing and gone to the restaurant's kitchen to see if we could have offered him something. To this day, I remember that man and wish I had said, "Please stay and have something, as my guest." I won't get that chance again. I still feel bad about it.

Working smart also means making sure you get something finished. I know plenty of people who use the excuse that they are perfectionists to explain why they neither start nor finish projects. Well, I am a perfectionist but I still get things done. The only way to do things is to do them well. Why waste your time on a halfhearted job? You won't get any satisfaction out of being mediocre. The saying "if something is worth doing, it's worth doing well" is so true. If for some reason you are not inspired to do something well, that might be a clue that either you don't like it or it simply is not worth doing. Don't be afraid to give up on a losing proposition. There is no shame in that. To me, there is much more shame in lending your name to and spending your time on something mediocre.

Since the time you have to complete anything is finite, it might help you to take a look at how much time you actually have and how you are using it. We spend a lot of time traveling to work by car or public transportation; we spend time getting ourselves organized to go to work; we spend time organizing our household. There is hardly such a thing as personal or family time now for most people. I am going to offer a radical suggestion about how to make more time.

Get up early. Yup, it's really that easy.

There's an old refrain in Spanish: *Dios ayuda al que madruga*, which means, "God helps the early riser." (There is also the English proverb "The early bird catches the worm," but I prefer the Spanish version. It's good to think there's a higher purpose at work.) Sleep is very important, but most people in good health don't need more than eight hours a night, if they even need that much. Of course, the other side of this particular coin is getting to bed at a reasonable hour to get your eight hours in.

It's been a long time since the sun beat me out of bed in the morning.

I get up at five a.m. every day of the year, weekends and holidays included. I've been doing this the better part of my life now, so in part I do it out of habit, and in part out of necessity. And I say "necessity" because those first moments all by myself help me determine how I will spend the rest of the day. The morning represents hope to me. I get up before the sun rises and I watch the day break. First thing, I spend some time in silence all by myself. The solitude allows me to think, reflect, appreciate, and to spend some time just being grateful. Then I quickly get to work. I make a lunch for our daughter, Emily, to take to school, I play with the dogs, I make breakfast, and then around six thirty I let the housekeeper in.

Getting up early means I have time to start my day with a routine that recharges my mental batteries. I get a jump on the day and put myself in an upbeat mood and a positive frame of mind. No matter how hectic or challenging the day is going to be, I always have the morning ritual. It also means I can plan my day and make a laundry list of what I want to accomplish. Here's where my focus on time management comes in again. As I see it, you've got one shot at each day. Days don't repeat themselves—they keep ticking off on the calendar whether you like it or not—so you really have to make the most of each and every one.

A normal day for me is hectic, filled with activity: meetings, people, noise, sound, problems, the unexpected, and fun. My day probably isn't different in that sense from your day. But how I begin it might just be, and I believe that what that time of the day represents for me is key to how I see my life and the way I live it.

Okay, maybe you don't want to get up that early in the morning. Perhaps you want to stay up late watching movies. If getting a lot of sleep is important to you, that's fine. But using time one way comes at the expense of something else. In the end, maybe you don't want to be an entrepreneur after all. Maybe you like listening to the radio all day and don't want the stress of running a company or of working long hours. There so are many trade-offs. If you don't like getting up early, if you value your sleep more than you do being the first at the office or opening the shop before the competition, that's fine. Be true to what you really want. But be prepared to think it through and accept the consequences. You likely won't be number one in what you do. You won't make as much money as you could, but that's okay. Money is not going to bring you happiness. It may make some things easier, but with a lot of money comes a lot of stress. But you can be perfectly happy with less material wealth than the other guy. On the other hand, if you are successful, wealthy, and happy, that's pretty amazing. Not too many people have won that particular trifecta.

Ultimately what you want to do is enjoy life and work is where we spend most of our lives. Fewer and fewer people seem to have the time to even enjoy leisure now. Some of that for sure has to do with the increased pressure and demands that our jobs place on us and the longer and longer distances people need to travel just to get to work. But a lot of it has to do with a bad use of time.

To counter that, identify what is important for you. And begin by sacrificing those activities that are getting in the way of your dedicating your time to what you love to do, on a personal and professional level. My time isn't any more elastic than anyone else's, but I use it well, and I always have.

WE'LL HAVE A LOT MORE to say on this subject later in the book, but it's important to identify treating people well as part of a work-smart strategy. It helps to think about the golden rule. Every major religion and philosophy has a version of this idea: Do unto others as you would have them do unto you. It pays off in life, and it's a smart business strategy as well. Remember, it begins and ends with you. Respect yourself, your own vision and talent, and the work that you do. Then extend that level of respect to everyone around you and all the people you deal with.

As far as other people are concerned, decency is the number one rule of engagement. You have to treat everyone with the same respect and kindness with which you wish to be treated, be they employees or the boss. There are people who have worked with me for well over twenty years. I keep them employed and they want to stay because we treat one another with a lot of respect.

It's important to act and make decisions every day that are consistent with your long-term strategies. That doesn't just mean thinking how much money you are going to make (though that's part of it, and that's a good part). You also have to be thinking about being in the game for a long time (there's that planning again!). That means taking good care of the people who work with you, and thinking about their well-being over the long term.

Treating people well develops a positive working environment, and you get the most out of people when you are kind to them. They become loyal to you, and in turn they are usually willing to happily go the extra mile and to work harder for you. Why? Because they see opportunity with you. Treating people decently doesn't just mean saying, "Good morning, how's the family?"—although, of course, that is fundamental. Treating people well means knowing where their talents and aspirations lie. When you know that, you can encourage them to take on other tasks and even try other positions in your company. Know the people you work with and invest time in them. Tell them they can do and be whatever they want to be. Make them a part of your life, your business, your dream. A true leader is someone who can get the best out of people. A company's people are its best resource, and again, you want to use your resources well.

If you instill a sense of ownership in your colleagues and employees, you will be infusing your workplace with a good attitude and a spirit of teamwork. Attitude, on all levels, is worth a lot—and it begins at the top. Consider the effect of good service at a restaurant. If you have a cheerful and attentive waiter, you might overlook any shortcomings in the food. But if it's the other way around—the food is hot and the waiter is cold— you are probably not going to go back to that restaurant. And the success of a restaurant, like many businesses, is in its loyal clientele, its repeat customers.

Treating people well will also earn you a reputation as a good person and boss. And never underestimate the value of a good reputation. A good reputation is vital to a successful business, and it bears repeating: A good reputation, which it may have taken years to establish, is easy to lose and extremely difficult to rebuild. Treating people well should be considered another element in a work-smart strategy.

CHAPTER FIFTEEN

Take Risks and Think Big

My parents and I began to settle into our lives together. I was busy with my job at Bacardi, my studies, and now playing gigs with the Miami Latin Boys, which was taking up more and more of my time. Our home was small and we knew that we would eventually need more space, especially since the plan to bring my brother and his family from Cuba had become the main driving force in our lives.

My father continued to play cards, and it seemed like he was winning a lot of the time. One weekend night I came home after playing with the band and I saw an enormous pile of dollars on top of the kitchen table. My father had obviously won big at a game. As I've said, it wasn't the money he cared about; he wanted to win so he could stay in the game. I set down my accordion case and stared at the money.

I could see what was going to happen to it. I could just imagine that my father would take that money and lose it in a game—if not one game then over the course of a couple of weeks. It hadn't been that long since he'd taken the stash of mine and gambled it away into nothing. My parents really needed to do something more productive with the money, I thought.

So I acted. I opened the accordion case, took out the instrument, and put it in my room. I then scooped up about half the money on the table and hid it inside the instrument case. I wasn't sure exactly what I was going to do with the money, but I knew that I wasn't going to let my dad lose it in a poker game.

As I suspected, my father didn't notice that about half his money was missing. I hung on to it until I could figure out what to do with it. Within a few weeks, I heard about an opportunity to buy a small clothing manufacturing business. Since my parents had already worked in this type of business, it struck me as the ideal opportunity for them. I bought the business, and my parents began working there—no questions asked!

I can still see them in my mind's eye, getting up at the crack of dawn and going off to work. Like so many immigrants, they worked hard at whatever honest work they could find, in order to contribute and to make better lives for themselves and for their children. They were a powerful example.

I took a gamble in buying the small business. But it was a calculated risk, certainly not the kind of gamble my father would have taken with the money. Sure enough, he didn't make his fortune with the money I left on the table that night. It wasn't the first risk I took, nor would it be the last by any stretch of the imagination. As the saying goes, fortune favors the brave. At certain points in your life you've just got to shut your eyes and go for it!

Working in a small business, especially when you're the owner, might be the very definition of risk. But at the time my investment fit into the larger plan. I was doing well enough financially. I still desperately wanted to get my brother and his family out of Cuba, but by this point, money alone wasn't enough. People just were not allowed to up and leave if they wanted to, and it would remain that way for a long time. But the risk I took with that money kept our family headed in the right direction.

Leaving Cuba in the first place had been a significant risk, because there was no guarantee of success. I didn't really think of my departure in those terms at the time, because the consequences of not taking that step were unthinkable to me. In one way I risked everything, because I might never have seen my mother again. I made a calculation (even if it was instantaneous!). That's the key thing to remember about taking risks—make sure they're calculated ones.

Look at it another way. I've already described how I felt responsible for my father at an early age, and said that feeling a sense of responsibility is an important part of being a successful entrepreneur. There is an important proviso: Take responsibility, but also take risks. I'm going to tell you over and over both to be a risk taker but also to be cautious. The message isn't contradictory. You have to make sacrifices in order to achieve your dreams, and that is where risk taking and caution meet.

Keep in mind that the decisions you make will determine your success or failure. Your decisions are yours and yours alone, no matter who is advising you. There is a very simple mantra here that bears repeating: responsibility, risk, reward.

Don't be paralyzed by the thought that you might fail at something. Failure is a part of life, and we can learn from our mistakes. Never be afraid to fail. The biggest failure is not trying at all. We all have failures in our lives. We just rarely talk about them. We live in a success-oriented society. But to succeed you have to fail at some point along the way. We learn so much from our failures and from life's bad experiences. It's unfortunate, but true. There's no such thing as a "bad experience" if you learn from it. Be persistent. Many failures are the result of giving up too early and too easily.

Part of reducing risks is by taking what you love and combining it with what you know. What if you have a degree in finance but love cooking? What's stopping you from running a restaurant? Is it the fear of failure or the thought that since you worked hard to get your finance degree you have to put it to good use? If the latter is the case, then make that degree work for you. But I would urge you to make sure you are following that course of action for the right reasons. Again, it's essential that you do what you love, but you can also be practical about that by using your knowledge and skills and experience to get you into the field that really excites you.

This is something you should continually evaluate in your working life. Many entrepreneurs have a fairly short attention span—some extremely short. As soon as they're successful, they want to move on to the next challenge. There's nothing wrong with that, of course—it shows ambition and enthusiasm—and it is probably part of the DNA of most entrepreneurs.

The current economy is full of challenges, which means that it's also full of opportunities if you're prepared to be creative and, yes, take a few risks. You may want to think twice before you leave a secure position to follow that dream you've been cultivating, but there are, unfortunately, millions of Americans who've been recently laid off who have relatively little to lose.

When you go to another country, as I did—and twice—it's only logical that you look for security, probably more security than people who have lived their whole lives in your new country. I did that. I looked for security from the outset. I started to work as soon as I could, right away, in fact. I was certainly motivated to seek security, and I still am. I found my security in a daytime job working for Bacardi. It was at night and on the weekends that I took my risks, by playing music.

With my day job, I knew I made enough money to cover my rent, food, and other necessities and to take care of my mom and dad until they got settled into a business of their own. My day job was my insurance, so to speak. An awareness of this need for security, which is more marked in people who don't have a safety net like a big extended family, has ironically allowed me to take more risks. I learned early on to bolster my situation by always doing more than satisfying my immediate needs.

My mother always had confidence in my abilities. She laid the groundwork for my plans. I always dreamed big, even when I was a boy in Santiago de Cuba and didn't know too much about the world beyond my own. No dream was ever unobtainable or too absurd. If I wanted to do something, I began by believing I could.

I've always tried to follow my mother's example by letting my kids think big for themselves. Gloria and I provide the framework for our kids to follow their own dreams.

Emily is now around the same age I was when I left Cuba with my father. She's a very talented drummer and guitarist. Think of a combination of Sheila E. (who's played with Gloria recently) and Carlos Santana! Gloria has been on her amazing 90 Millas tour for much of the last two

years, and we went all over Spain, as well as Holland, England, and Ireland, before selling out huge arenas in South America—Uruguay, Chile,
Argentina, Peru, Ecuador.

The reception Gloria and the band got at the concerts you had to see
to believe. The shows were three hours of joy. A highlight for us was
when Emily would come to the front of the stage and play a guitar solo,
or crash and roll though a spectacular set on the drums. She's amazing.
Fearless. I've been performing in front of crowds for forty years, but
some of these crowds were as big as any I've ever seen. I always trick myself into thinking the gig's not that big by picking out a friendly face in
the crowd and sticking with him or her through the concert.

It takes guts to stand up in front of thousands of people and play, especially when you're fourteen years old. It's a risk. You're making yourself vulnerable, exposing your talent to the world when you never know
how they are going to react. I think a key thing for Emily is that because
her family's there with her onstage, she feels secure.

Finding security, especially in the ones you love, makes risk taking a
lot easier.

CHAPTER SIXTEEN

Find Your Own Rhythm

T hank God there is no recipe for success! How boring would that be? We all have to blaze our own trails. So much of our future success depends on who we are and often also on where we come from—be it a place, a family, or a particular situation. Of course, luck can also play a huge role. And you also have to recognize a good thing when you see it.

My big break as a musician—and as a man—came when I saw this lovely girl get up and sing at a wedding. Gloria Fajardo was very poised onstage but very shy off it. In fact, it was easier to get her to join the band than it was to get her to become my girlfriend—that took a couple more years. Gloria and her cousin Merci Murciano often sang together, so when I invited Gloria to try out for our band, the Miami Latin Boys, she asked if her cousin could come along. I hired the two of them, and I re-named the group the Miami Sound Machine. This was 1976.

By that time the Miami Latin Boys were one of the city's top local bands. The band was really hot. Miami had changed dramatically in the previous decade, in part because of an economic boom but also because of the huge influx of Cubans and other immigrants from Latin America. That Latin population provided the Miami Latin Boys with a ready-made audience. But since I had also spent part of my teenage years in the United States, listening to the great pop and rock of the era—like just about everyone else my age in Miami—I also wanted to sing in English.

There were some other acts that came to the forefront at the same time, but our fusion of Latin with Anglo was unique. We listened to the great artists of Motown, like Smokey Robinson, Stevie Wonder, and the Jacksons, and also British Invasion bands like the Beatles, the Stones. We mixed that with the music we'd grown up listening to in Cuba and the songs that the expatriates in Miami loved to listen to, until we could turn our hand to anything. Gloria has said I used to play "The Hustle" (Van McCoy's huge 1975 disco hit) on the accordion, if you can picture that. The fusion of Cuba and America was what we called the Miami sound. And so, Miami Sound Machine.

Our success was a combination of timing, talent, and luck. And again, of recognizing a good thing when it came along.

We became very adept at tailoring our performances to our various audiences, mixing Latin standards with English-language pop, or playing just Latin standards or just pop—whatever we figured the audience wanted to hear. While that mix added to our popularity, being true to ourselves and singing the music we loved was at the core of it.

We became so well-known locally that I was asked at one point to go listen to a group and to give them some pointers. A few months later, the Miami Latin Boys were playing at a wedding and a girl came up to me in the hallway during a break and told me that I'd given her and her friends some tips on improving their performance. I invited the girl to join us onstage for a number, and at first she said no. Her mother, who was standing behind her, said, "Go on, Gloria. You sing beautifully." Gloria Fajardo sat in for one number and did so very well. She enjoyed herself so much she stayed for several more songs.

At the time when we met at the wedding, Gloria was studying psychology at the University of Miami. She was an exceptional student—she finished her degree with a double major in just three years—and while at the university she also worked full-time at Miami International Airport as an interpreter. Gloria already spoke fluent Spanish, English, and French.

Gloria seemed like a normal seventeen-year-old girl: hardworking, serious, devoted to her family. The first things I noticed about her were her beautiful eyes and lovely skin, and also her shyness—Gloria is surprisingly shy, especially for someone who is a performer who can hold a crowd of fifty thousand captive with a song. I was intrigued, but she was very young and extremely serious, so I certainly did not think about her in romantic terms. My first feelings toward her were ones of respect, and as I got to know her and her story better I felt enormous admiration. She is the hardest-working person I know, and she always has been like that.

Gloria's life and mine had some definite similarities. We were both born in Cuba, and we loved music, family, and hard work. And both of our young lives had been marked by long periods of separation from ones we loved, in my case, from my mother; in Gloria's, it was her father.

Gloria's parents, Jose Manuel Fajardo and Gloria Garcia, met and married in Havana in 1956. Jose was a motorcycle policeman and later a motorcycle escort for the wife of Cuba's then-president, Fulgencio Batista. Gloria's mother was a kindergarten teacher, and she valued education above just about anything. Gloria was born September 1, 1957, a year after her parents married. They had a comfortable life in the Miramar neighborhood of Havana, living in a house next door to Gloria's grandparents.

It was not long, however, before their lives, like so many others, were turned upside down with the arrival of Fidel Castro to power on January 1, 1959. In their case, because of Jose Manuel's job, change came about very quickly and abruptly.

Anyone associated with the previous government was considered suspect. Many were detained and thrown in jail, including Jose Manuel.

The new government was repressive from the word "go." They not only arrested people and held them without charging them; they executed people. They started taking possession of houses and other privately owned properties. They closed casinos and brothels and even the national lottery, and they fired people from government jobs and the military.

After Jose Manuel was released, things went from bad to worse. At that point, Gloria and Jose Manuel decided they needed to get out of Cuba "until things blew over." They, like many others, were confident that this repressive regime did not have staying power and would soon be replaced.

So like so many just before them, Gloria and young Gloria—who was only two years old at the time—flew into exile in Miami. It was May 1960.

Jose Manuel joined them a month later. They had very little money, spoke virtually no English, and they had not had a lot of life experience. But they did have a community, one to which they would contribute and on which they would depend. It is in these exile communities that immigrants find security.

The family had barely settled into exile when Jose Manuel went off to train for a secret mission. That was the failed Bay of Pigs Invasion, which took place in April 1961. Jose Manuel survived but was taken prisoner by the Castro forces.

Many of the other families in their neighborhood near Miami's Orange Bowl were in the same situation as the Fajardos. The women all helped one another out as much as they could. These were especially rough periods for families. The Cuban revolution had caused many kinds of separation—mine from my mother and Gloria's from her father. We coped with them in different ways, but as Gloria herself said, the stress of these times caused kids like her and me to grow up very quickly, as Gloria's mother found out.

Gloria had told little Glorita that her father was "away, working on a farm." She did not want to scare Glorita, and she thought she was too young to understand what the situation really was. Until one day she overheard Glorita say to someone, "My dad is in jail, but don't tell my mom; she thinks he's on a farm."

Gloria's mother says that she herself grew up overnight. She decided to create a happy home for her Glorita (as she was called in the family), even if the circumstances were grim and uncertain. Of the few things Gloria's mother was able to bring out of Cuba were albums—Celia Cruz and Joselito were favorites. The house didn't have much, but it always had music. Glorita grew up with her mother's passion for music, and her mother taught her all she could about Cuban culture. As it was for me, music was always at the center of Glorita's life.

What's at the center of your life?

CHAPTER SEVENTEEN

Be Well Accompanied

W hatever you do in this life, it will be pretty rare that you do it alone. Work, family, leisure—they all usually involve other people. In my case, I have had someone by my side for most of my adult life who has accompanied me well. And I have accompanied Gloria very well in her joys and difficulties. There is so much more to relationships than just luck. There is hard work, and especially there is respect. Knowing that person and his or her personal story and ambitions, where they came from and who they truly are—all those are key to successful partnerships and relationships, be they business or romantic (or both!).

As I've said, life was especially hard for Gloria's family. For a year and a half after the Bay of Pigs Invasion in which he participated, Gloria's father Jose Manuel and 1,112 other men were held in Cuban jails until they were released in exchange for a U.S. government–sponsored ransom of $53 million in food and medical supplies. He and his comrades returned to the United States on Christmas Day, 1962, and within weeks Jose Manuel decided to enlist in the U.S. Army. He told his wife that the United States was fighting communism in Vietnam, and he was willing to fight communism anywhere in the world. He enlisted, and the family moved several times over the next few years to different military bases in Texas and South Carolina. When he was deployed to Vietnam,

99

Gloria and her daughters (they had now had their second child, Rebecca—Becky) returned to Miami.

When Jose Manuel returned from Vietnam in 1967, he was sent to the Panama Canal zone. It wasn't long after he returned from Panama that he began to show symptoms of what was later diagnosed as multiple sclerosis. The family believes that Jose Manuel was exposed in Vietnam to Agent Orange, the highly toxic herbicide U.S. forces used to defoliate Communist-controlled areas to deny food and cover. He was soon honorably discharged.

His discharge began a long battle that changed all their lives. The disease progressed rapidly, and Jose Manuel was soon unable to walk, much less work outside of the home. Gloria would now be the main breadwinner and head of the household, and a lot of the burden of taking care of the house and the younger child fell to young Glorita, a heavy burden for someone not yet in her teens.

Like me, as a young person Glorita sought refuge in music. During the times her father was away from the family, which was much of her childhood, Glorita would record herself playing guitar and singing old standards, and she would mail those tapes to her father. Her mother encouraged her to sing for her friends, and although Glorita was very shy, she was always eager to please her mother, and she would sing and play guitar.

By the time Gloria was seventeen, her father's condition had deteriorated so badly that he was admitted to a veterans' administration hospice, where he remained for the rest of his life.

Gloria finished high school at the top of her class and won a scholarship to the University of Miami, where she majored in psychology and communications and minored in French. It was at this point in her life that she entered my life.

After her performance with the Miami Latin Boys at the wedding, I asked her if she'd like to join the band. I explained that I had been thinking about adding a female voice to the mix, and that although we didn't make much money performing, we did it because we loved it. I also told her that we took it seriously, something she would understand right away.

I could see that she was keen to sing with us, but she was hesitant. She said she would be able to sing only on weekends, and that she could perform with the band only as long as she kept up her grades at the university, which was very important to her. She also asked if she could bring her cousin to the next rehearsal, explaining that the two of them often sang and played guitar together. Yes, I said, but they would have to share their earnings.

Gloria was accompanied by her mother, her sister, and her grandmother to the first rehearsal. Of course, she was a good Cuban girl and she wasn't going to go off unaccompanied with strange men. And of course I understood and respected that. Her cousin Merci came to the second rehearsal. Merci and Gloria joined the band at first as backup singers, but it soon became obvious to me that Gloria could take a more prominent role.

We needed something that reflected who we were. We were a bunch of immigrant kids who loved where we came from but had also embraced American music. We were Miami. So we became the Miami Sound Machine. I couldn't think of a more fitting name for who we were and what we were doing.

Gloria's charisma was evident from the outset. Despite her shyness, she connected with the audience. She truly enjoyed performing, although at first she often gazed down at the stage floor—maybe people also considered that part of her charm! We started to work closely together to improve her stage presence. I told Gloria to pretend she was singing to me in the living room, something that came easily to her. I saw so much potential in her as a performer. At one point, I even told her that she could improve herself 95 percent. (She told me a few years later, "So at the time you only liked five percent of me?")

Gloria worked very hard to improve herself, and her efforts helped to transform the band. It wasn't traditional to have a female lead singer as part of a Latin band, but I also didn't see us as a traditional band. We were part of something new, something transformative. We brought the best of our musical traditions and blended them with the best of American and British pop. That was how we saw ourselves.

My feelings toward Gloria were also changing and growing the more time we spent together. I told my mother when I met Gloria that I was not going to start a romance with her unless I was serious. From what I knew of Gloria's life story, she had gone through too much to be involved in something frivolous. Because I admired her so much I wasn't going to ruin things, and of course we also worked together. Besides, I don't believe in love at first sight; love grows.

The summer of 1976, we were playing a July Fourth concert on a ship. I knew my feelings for Gloria and I decided to express them. I told her it was my birthday (not true!) and I asked her for a kiss. She laughed and said, "No, I'll get you a present." I persisted, saying, "Just a kiss on the cheek." When she moved in to kiss me on the cheek, I turned and we kissed. And so it began.

My parents loved Gloria immediately, of course. Gloria's grandmother, whom she was very close to, loved me immediately too. Gloria's mother, on the other hand, was not crazy about me, to put it mildly. She had brought up Gloria very strictly, insisting she finish her university education, and I was hardly what Gloria Fajardo had envisioned for her daughter. She was worried that I was just a musician, and that our music wasn't going to take us anywhere. As far as she was concerned, playing music wasn't an appropriate or very secure way to make a living.

I was determined to prove Gloria's mother wrong, of course, because I was and am a serious professional and family man. Even before Gloria and I dated, I always respected Gloria's mother's rules and her values, but despite that respect, winning her over was not going to be easy. I decided the only thing I could do was to continue to be true to my own values. She would eventually come around. But in the end, my relationship was with Gloria, not her mother.

A few days before Valentine's Day, 1978, Gloria was at the house I had bought and shared with my parents. I had bought an engagement ring and was planning to give it to her on Valentine's Day and to ask her to marry me. But I couldn't wait. Gloria was sitting talking to my mother when I pulled the small blue box out of my pocket and handed it to her.

She opened it and laughed, and threw her arms around my mother! The two of them hugged, and then she hugged me.

Gloria graduated with honors from the University of Miami that spring, and although she had been accepted to study at the Sorbonne in Paris, and also the clinical school in psychology at the University of Miami, she opted to throw in her lot with me and our music, 100 percent. We began to plan our wedding, and although I wanted a big party with an orchestra to celebrate our union, Gloria's mother put her foot down. By this time Jose Manuel's condition was grave, and she insisted that it would not be appropriate to party while Gloria's father was dying. I agreed, although, I admit it, reluctantly.

We married on September 2, 1978, a day after Gloria's twenty-first birthday. Gloria entered the church by herself. She said that no man was worthy of taking her father's place in escorting her down the aisle. The same priest who had married Gloria's parents in Havana performed the ceremony. He stepped away from the altar and brought her the last few steps to me. The Mass was beautiful in its simplicity, exactly what we wanted. After the ceremony, Gloria and I slipped away quietly to visit her father in the hospice. Jose Manuel had not spoken in many, many months, but when Gloria entered his room in her wedding dress, he looked at her and said, "Glorita." It was the blessing we both so wanted.

It is a blessing that has accompanied us as we have accompanied each other.

CHAPTER EIGHTEEN

Expect Resistance and
Prepare Yourself for It

F ast-forward a few years, to 1984. I'm sitting in the lobby of the CBS Building in New York City, watching people get into and out of elevators, and hugging a tape canister to me. I've flown up to New York from Miami to try to get the promotions people at our record label to listen to one of Miami Sound Machine's songs and to get behind it. I was certain we had a big hit on our hands, but I had a lot of work to do to convince our label. And I could stay only that day. I had to get back to Miami.

We had been singing in Spanish for years, covering songs of traditional Cuban music as well as performing our own material, first as the Miami Latin Boys and then as the Miami Sound Machine. Our first album was *Renacer* (*Live Again*, 1977), which was released on a small local label. The album was half in English and half in Spanish. Even though we were all Spanish speakers in the band, we considered ourselves Americans and English speakers as well. And although we had no intention of leaving our beloved roots behind, we knew we could do so much more. Singing in English and covering the great pop tunes of our day were also very much a part of who we were. We were really the first bilingual group out there.

In 1978 and 1979 we recorded two more albums—*Miami Sound Machine* and *Imported*, respectively. We financed all of our early recordings at a cost of about $2,000 per song, which allowed us to do about one take and the mixing. (We were later reimbursed when we were signed by the label, but we did have to front the initial costs ourselves.) We also marketed those two albums locally ourselves. In 1980, Discos CBS International—a division of CBS that was based in Miami—signed us to record Spanish-language albums for its worldwide Latin markets. Even though CBS initially wanted us to record in only Spanish and for markets abroad, I saw this as an incredible opportunity to break into the broader U.S. market. Not only would we eventually begin recording in English, I figured, but the U.S. market would soon be clamoring for music in Spanish and for Latin rhythms.

CBS rereleased our previous recordings, which went to the top of the charts throughout Latin America. Signing with a record label seemed to be the boost and the support we needed. But I also knew that I couldn't leave all the work to the record company. We knew what we wanted to do with our music and also how we wanted to market it. I was determined to have a very proactive relationship with CBS. We visited the record company all the time to keep ourselves on their radar.

Over the next few years, we recorded three more albums with CBS: *Otra Vez* (*Another Time*), *Rio* (*River*), and *A Toda Máquina* (*At Full Speed*). We toured Latin America, the markets where those albums were released, and they all made it to the top of the charts. Touring was fun, grueling, hectic, and ultimately tremendously rewarding. In Miami, we had become used to performing in venues of twenty-five hundred seats, maximum. In Latin America we did festivals and concerts for massive crowds—we routinely sold out soccer stadiums of thirty or forty thousand fans.

The demands of touring took their toll on some of the band members. We had jelled as a group. Miami Sound Machine was made up of Marcos Avila, who played bass, Kiki Garcia (drums), and Raul Murciano (keyboards and saxophone). Gloria and I weren't the only couple in the band—Gloria's cousin Merci and Raul had fallen in love and gotten married as well. Just as things were heating up, though, Raul and I had an argument—he wanted to do more Anglo music—and he and

Merci decided to quit the Miami Sound Machine. I also found it diffi-cult to travel as much with the band as I needed to because of my com-mitment at Bacardi, where I had joined the Latin marketing department. Also, it was difficult to perform and manage the band at the same time, so I stopped performing, and Gloria began to take an even more promi-nent role during concerts.

Our contract with Discos CBS International was up, but not over, because we were picked up by Epic, an even bigger label that was part of the CBS empire at the time (Epic is now owned by Sony). We were writing more and more of our own material and wanted to record in English, not abandoning our Spanish-language fan base but incorporat-ing a new, bigger one.

Over the course of a few good years playing and recording we had refined our sound into what I call Latin pop—a blend of Latin rhythms and pop, salsa, and disco, with lyrics in Spanish and now in English. It was our identity, but what was so gratifying for us was that so many other people identified with our sound. Our fans were mainly other La-tinos, but we could already see how popular our sound was with people who were open to something different, yet familiar at the same time.

When we wrote "Dr. Beat," though, both Gloria and I thought that was a song that should stay in English. This was the song I wanted the promotion people to get behind on my visit to New York. The record company wanted to release a single of our song "Luchare" and had agreed to put "Dr. Beat" on the B side, which is limbo for a song. For the label, "Dr. Beat" was too much of a departure from our usual material. For us, it was part of our sound. It was unique, it was new, and we be-lieved it would appeal to a wider audience. When we played the song live, audiences loved it. Something about it touched them, and it cut across racial and ethnic lines. The sound wasn't popular just with Latino audiences, but with black and Anglo ones as well. The problem was that it was a totally new sound for the industry, and the company didn't know what to do with it, which meant they didn't know how to promote it. They didn't want to back it the way we thought it needed to be promoted.

But we persisted. We were absolutely convinced that our Latin pop—and "Dr. Beat"—would have universal appeal. It became my job to make the record label executives see that my idea was a great one, that it would be popular, and that it would sell. I had to make my enthusiasm contagious; I had to be sure of myself and my project. I had to be persistent. I didn't come to New York to take "no" for an answer.

As it turned out, I didn't exactly get a direct "no"; I just got the run-around. "He'll be with you shortly," followed by, "He's busy; come back tomorrow." I knew where all that was headed, and besides, I couldn't come back tomorrow—I had taken a day off, and only one day off, to go to New York. I couldn't even stay the night. I had to fly back to Miami that evening and get back to work in the morning.

If you'd have told me at that point that years later I'd be appointed president of the equivalent company as I was with Sony, I'd have asked you what you were smoking. It would have been hard to imagine years later such a different scene in that lobby. "Oh, Mr. Estefan, let me get the elevator for you." Back then it was, "He's busy; come back tomorrow."

I had known even before I went to New York that the record label was resistant to promoting a song of ours in English. They had pigeon-holed us and figured that our audience was Spanish speaking and didn't want to hear songs in English, and also that English speakers wouldn't be interested in what they perceived was a Latin group. I knew—I *knew* in my head, heart, and bones—that that just wasn't so.

I flew back to Miami, not with my mission accomplished, but certainly not with my hopes deflated either. I don't know why people are so resistant to new ideas, but you know what? They are. That shouldn't stop you, though. I am remembering that trip to New York now as I think about how often you are going to meet resistance when you're trying to sell someone on your idea. It doesn't matter how great it is.

It would be easier sometimes to just hear an outright "no." Actually, you'll be lucky at times if you even get someone to listen to your pitch. So, does that mean you should give up? There are a few cast-iron rules that you can follow when your idea is stalled, whether it's a great song or a new formula for window-washing fluid.

The first thing is that you're going to meet resistance, as we did. It takes people time to get used to something new. Remember, the Beatles were turned down. The Beatles! There's no simple recipe for getting what you want and for convincing others that your idea needs to be pursued. Meeting resistance of one kind or another is almost inevitable, and you have to deal with it. It might be something you can change, something you have to live with, or something you can go around. Just so that you don't get easily discouraged or have the wrong kind of expectations, accept the fact that you will almost always encounter resistance of one kind or another.

There are always going to be two forces at work: the internal and the external. Us and them. I don't say that so that you develop a "me against the world" attitude. I say that so that you always keep in mind what you are up against. The external forces are much harder to control, so let's look first at you, the internal force. The place to begin is with self-assurance. Your belief in your great idea and your dream has to be rock-solid.

Start by saying "yes" to yourself and your own ideas. This means you need to begin with a positive attitude. As I've said already, this is the starting point for everything in life. I believe that being positive is at least as infectious as being negative, and you really can change the climate around you with a positive outlook. You can't always choose whom you do business with, but, believe me, you can change people, often by changing their negative attitudes and frame of mind.

I wish I could boil down the message in this chapter to, "Be positive," but the truth is, it's more accurate to say, "Don't be negative or allow others to be negative." If you've worked to make a positive attitude as habitual as breathing, then this will come naturally to you. It is exactly at this point, when you are meeting resistance to your new ideas, that your positive attitude will prove itself most valuable.

You also have to be original. Never imitate; create! Most people like to follow others, and they lack originality. It's not true that there is nothing new under the sun. And if you think there is nothing new under the sun, you'll never make it big. One of the advantages of coming to a new country and culture as I did is that everything seems so different, so new, so fresh, and yet you bring your own culture and background with you, which is new to others. It's at that place where ideas collide and are brought together that there's often great creativity.

The tendency just to follow the tried and true makes me think that people are afraid of anything different. I know that there is a natural resistance to change. Most people don't like to leave their comfort zone. And because of that they are also afraid of risks. Don't be one of those people. Be open to your own ideas and those of others.

Most of the things that really do work and that really are attractive to people—be they consumers or audiences—are new ideas. And yet, there is often so much resistance to trying anything original. You know, 99.9 percent of the people you run an original idea by will tell you, "That's not going to work." We were told "Dr. Beat" had too much trumpet, too much percussion. Well, don't tell me no! That's where intuition comes in. That's why you have to believe in your idea and yourself and listen to that little voice that tells you, "Yes, this is a great idea. I love it and so will other people."

Entrepreneurial people are the game changers. We are people who feel an irrepressible need to develop new ideas. We need to *create*. We're original. We're innovative. Well, we're swimming against the current when we start out, because so many times investors, or even just people we float our ideas by, think that the tried and true is the only way to go. Why do people want to be predictable in music, clothes, design, food, and other areas? The predictable often doesn't work either, maybe for the obvious reason that it's already on the market. While being original involves risk taking, being predictable is not always safe, either.

You have to fight against hearing that something is not going to work, that it's not going to happen, that "people are not used to that." As a composer and producer, I've always been driven to implement my own sounds and my own rules. That is where being from somewhere else can become a great advantage. You're different and people notice it right away. If you treat being different as the positive force that it really is, then you can go places.

CHAPTER NINETEEN

Do It Yourself!

I won't deny that as I flew back from New York to Miami that day I felt discouraged. Of course I did. But I also took stock of all that I had, and at that moment my belief that we had a hit song with "Dr. Beat" was the biggest thing I had going. I wasn't going to waste the opportunity. The promotions people weren't the only folks who knew how to market. After all, I had been working in the Latin marketing department at Bacardi, so I knew something about the art of promotion myself.

Help from the record label was the obvious way to start, but it wasn't the only way. I had taken a much larger role in the management side of the band. If you want to think big, to revise the definition of your own success upward and replan your life positively and ambitiously, then you have to grab the reins and do it yourself. You can't rely on anyone else to do it. It doesn't matter if you have a giant multinational company like a record label working for you; you have to take the initiative.

Gloria became pregnant with our first child the same year we signed with CBS. There was an awful lot happening in our lives around that time, that's for sure. I can still see Gloria, with her big belly, visiting not just the CBS offices but also visiting the loading docks and talking to the folks who were physically handling our albums. One of the keys to success in the music business has always been distribution. Back then in the predigital era it was about getting your records into the stores. It's a little different now, of course. Anyone with an Internet connection can get access to songs. It's a question of getting people to pay for them.

Nayib was born September 2, 1980, our second wedding anniversary. It seemed our happiness was complete. Little did we know how much more was to come.

Having a child didn't cramp our style at all. In fact, Nayib turned out to be highly portable, as are many children when you start including them in your life and work early on. He came to rehearsals and recordings and even toured with us. My mother was an extraordinary help to us with Nayib. She was more than a grandmother; she became a second mother to him, and all our lives were much richer for that. More often than not, Nayib traveled with us. But when he didn't, he stayed with my parents.

As I mentioned, after a couple of years I stopped performing and took over the management of the band. I had to leave my position at Bacardi because I couldn't juggle everything successfully anymore. It was time to commit myself to making a success of the music business full-time.

While the music business has changed an incredible amount in the last ten, fifteen years, our experience in the early days is instructive to someone heading out into the music business today. The best advice is being hands-on and trying to make sure you are in control. Learning to budget will be the most valuable skill you acquire. Before we signed with CBS we didn't have much choice, paying for our own recordings. On our third record we got $3,000 from the record company, I think, and paid the rest of the $20,000 ourselves. The marketing was up to us.

This is a good time to pause and reflect on how things have changed. The challenges are different from twenty and even ten years ago. Today young performers are often entirely on their own. Sales of blank CDs outstrip sales of prerecorded discs. Even if you take into account rising digital sales, total album sales in all formats fell 10 percent in 2008. Big retailers like the Virgin Megastores are gone. Even if concert ticket revenues went up in 2008 they were skewed by the higher-priced big-name events. An artist like Gloria who has been established for years can tour, of course, but if you're just starting out you need to establish yourself first before you can go out on the road. There are a lot of misconceptions about what record labels can do nowadays. It's almost impossible to get the backing of a record label when they have declining sales, and have no A and R budget and basically no money. I think record labels will disappear partly because they have made the mistake of not putting creative folks in charge. But that void is creating an opportunity for young artists. Eventually there will be electronic labels based on the Internet, and today's artist needs to be ready for that. You have to be your own label and promoter. Distribution has pretty much disappeared, but the Internet offers extraordinary opportunities that we didn't have.

After we got nowhere with the label, we got to work on "Dr. Beat." As soon as I got back to Miami, my secretary and I began taking the record to radio stations and clubs. Clubs are always looking for something new to put on their turntables, and they were pretty receptive to our sound. We were encouraged as we saw the reaction every time a deejay would play "Dr. Beat." The dance floor would fill and people would sing along.

We had done our bit by getting the song out there; now it was just a question of time before the right person heard it. Sure enough, before long a visitor from England heard "Dr. Beat" in a club on Miami Beach and took the record back to the U.K. Soon it was a hit—number one in the clubs!—on the other side of the Atlantic. That was really our big break. We had begun the crossover by crossing over the Atlantic. People started calling the record companies in the U.S. saying, "There's this great new sound; you've gotta sign this band." Well, they already had us; they just didn't know what they had! It started for us in England, and in Holland too, and we never forget that. Gloria played the U.K. and the Netherlands on her most recent tour, and the fans are great to us over there.

There was luck involved, to be sure, but there was also the belief in our sound, originality, and persistence. And it all began to pay off very quickly. The record company decided to back up the hit by sending us on tour to Europe, and soon "Dr. Beat" topped the dance charts all over Europe. We knew what touring was like, because we'd already toured extensively in Central and South America, where we had already gained a large following.

As exhausting as touring can be, we knew that this trip to Europe was a huge break on many levels. Touring puts you in contact with new audiences, and there is also a freedom to try out new material and to gauge reaction to it. The reaction of the audience can inspire you. It's like a pat on the back or the seal of approval for the work you are doing. The immediate positive reaction—provided it is positive, of course—brings instant gratification.

Our experience with "Dr. Beat" was extremely instructive on so many levels. The bottom line is that we worked hard to come up with a winning formula with Miami Sound Machine over a period of years of making music. We'd recorded seven albums! Sometimes it takes years to become an overnight success. Sure, we got lucky when the record was picked up in the U.K., but if we hadn't worked at pushing the single independently of our record label, no one would have been in a position to pick up the song. We worked hard to realize our dreams, we never gave up, and in the end we made our own luck.

THE FIRST FEW YEARS OF our marriage were a very busy time for us, personally as well as professionally. The year after we married, Gloria and I traveled to Cuba to see my brother and his family. This was the first time I had visited Cuba since I had left in 1967.

In 1979, Gloria and I flew to Havana and then took a long trip overland to see the family in Santiago. By the time we arrived in the city, we were physically exhausted. I hadn't seen my brother and my niece for twelve years, and I had never met my nephew. A lot had changed in their lives. My sister-in-law had died, and life was difficult for them even though my brother had a good job as a professor of solar energy at the University of Santiago.

I cannot adequately express both the joy and the sadness I felt at seeing my brother. I had worried that we would never see each other again, but there he was in flesh and blood, with my dear niece and nephew. And yet, I couldn't get them out of the country. Cuban citizens were still not allowed to simply leave, and since my brother had very publicly stated his intention to get away, government officials were making his life miserable. It would still be almost another two years before we would be able to get them out of Cuba.

When our family was still separated, my mother would not allow us to celebrate Christmas or birthdays. She always said that she could not enjoy those celebrations when she knew that her son and grandchildren in Cuba were being deprived. Gloria changed that in our lives, though. She insisted that we celebrate and that we enjoy and that we show gratitude for what we have. It was actually easier for me to think along those lines, in the hope that soon my brother and his family would be rejoining us.

During a speech the following year, Fidel Castro said that all those who wanted to leave the island could. This precipitated the huge Mariel Boatlift period in 1980, during which 125,000 Cubans arrived in south Florida. I rented a boat to go and get my brother and his family. But when I got to Cuba, we found out that they were not allowed to leave. I headed home dejected and got lost at sea for several days. It was a terrible time for our family on both sides of the Florida Straits, because no one had any word of me. And this coincided with Gloria's pregnancy with Nayib. I eventually made it home, but without my brother my mission was incomplete.

Still, there was another way, as there usually is. Since there were still no direct flights to the United States, my brother and his family had to leave via another country, just as the rest of us had. They eventually left Cuba for Costa Rica, where they stayed for several months before we were finally able to get them into the United States. I cannot tell you the joy and relief we all felt at that point.

(Life can also be full of sadness: Around this same time, Gloria's father, Jose Manuel, died. He had lived a short life, much of it, especially the final thirteen years, marred by his terrible illness. But he left a profound impression on those who knew him and even those who later came to hear the story of his courage and bravery.)

Having my brother and his family with us was a dream come true. A dream we had all struggled years to achieve. I figured I must have spent about six hours a day, what with second jobs and other efforts, all those years just working to get us all together again. Anything that lay ahead had to be easier than what we had lived through when we were apart.

Our family was together at last in freedom.

I had finally completed the task I set myself as a boy in Havana those many years before.

CHAPTER TWENTY

Turn "No" into "Yes"

T he success of "Dr. Beat" helped us convince the record execs to let us record an English-only album. That album, *Eyes of Innocence*, was our first major foray into the mainstream U.S. and European markets. Around the time of that album, we met three guys whom we were very keen to work with. Rafael Vigil, Joe Galdo, and Lawrence Dermer had already produced Latin music, so I felt confident they got what we wanted to do, and that they understood our sound. I hired them to co-produce our next album, *Primitive Love*, in 1985. This album was also all in English.

Before concerts in Europe we would play taped music of Cuban and Latin music as a warm-up. The European audiences were phenomenal—so open and receptive to our sound. Our confidence grew. One day while on tour, before *Eyes of Innocence* came out, when we were traveling from the Netherlands to the United Kingdom, Gloria said, "We should do a conga, but in English." At that point we had only two songs we played in English.

The conga is a very Cuban rhythm, with the long lines everyone's familiar with, where people move in time to the beating drums and fling out a leg to the fourth beat. We all loved the idea and started horsing around with, "Come on everybody, baby, do the conga. . . ." The song "Conga" was born. In English. And with our sound: horns and the

Cuban tumbao beat and some R & B thrown in. We loved it and we identified with it, which is what is most important to begin with.

But can you believe that again the record company thought it wouldn't work? "Radio won't play this," we heard. Wrong again. The song caught fire so quickly that it almost promoted itself. It was included on the sound track of the popular 1986 TV movie *Club Med* (which sure didn't hurt). It became a signature song—the first of many. We've seen people dance that song all over the world for twenty-five years.

"Conga" was the big hit from *Primitive Love* and our biggest hit ever. It was the ultimate crossover song—it zoomed into *Billboard* magazine's top ten, and it remains the only song ever to hit *Billboard*'s pop, soul, dance, and Latin charts simultaneously. At this point, Gloria was clearly the front man, or front woman in this case, of the band. And there were more changes in the works. Longtime member Marcos Avila decided to leave the band. He was recently married and he didn't want to travel as much. Marcos left on good terms, and he and his wife, journalist Cristina Saralegui, remain our close friends to this day. But his departure was another that began to change the DNA of the band for good.

Miami Sound Machine appeared at the record company's annual convention and we were asked to play "Conga." The execs were so pleased with the enthusiastic reception the record had received all over the world that, true to form, they asked us for a sequel, a kind of "Conga II." But we had already done "Conga," and Gloria had a ballad in mind. We insisted that "Words Get in the Way" was as much a part of our sound as "Conga" and "Dr. Beat" were. Again, persistence paid off and "Words Get in the Way" zoomed to the top of the charts. That was quickly followed by "Bad Boys"—not a Latin sound so much as a boppy, catchy tune. By this point, after a quick succession of hits, the record company's resistance was pretty well worn down. They could see that we had broken the mold for Latin groups and that, just as I had been saying all along, audiences would be really receptive.

We had won an important battle against external resistance. And one victory often paves the way for future ones. Why? Because you begin to develop a track record and you can take that to the bank. So the first victories are really important ones. But, despite success, you will continue to face resistance internally, with colleagues and even yourself.

Life was good. Even at this fairly early point, we had earned more money than we could have imagined, we had crossed over into the U.S. general market, and our families were well and prospering. Offers began to pour in. I started to diversify and to produce other artists, and Gloria was offered acting roles. (She was asked to appear on *Miami Vice*, which was the most popular show on TV at the time. Because it depicted our hometown as violent and as a haven for drug criminals, Gloria turned down the role.) Gloria's first major endorsement was with Pepsi, which paid her $1 million to sing in their commercials.

We had also already made some investments and now decided to form our own company to look after our holdings. In 1986, Estefan Enterprises was incorporated. We also moved into our dream house on Star Island, an island in Miami's Biscayne Bay. We built that house, and even though building a home is usually a source of stress for most people, I really enjoyed the process. I found architecture and design to be just another outlet for creativity. And of course, I had the best people working on the project, including my brother, Papo, who oversaw the construction and engineering. Gloria insisted we include an elevator in the house even though we were all young and the house was only two stories. She later told me that she thought about her father and his illness, and how hard it would have been for someone infirm or disabled to live in that or any house with a staircase. She thought someone in our family would need to use the elevator, and in fact it turned out to be her.

Our next album in 1987, *Let It Loose*, showcased the new composition of the group. The billing, for the first time, was Gloria Estefan and the Miami Sound Machine. The album had a slew of top hits, including "1-2-3," "Anything for You," "Rhythm Is Gonna Get You," and "Can't Stay away from You." We launched a worldwide tour for the next twenty months to support the album.

What an exciting time! I can still remember going to the Grammy show that year as if it were yesterday. It was one of the most thrilling nights of my career and my life. I remember seeing so many greats there whom I had so long admired, like Quincy Jones, Stevie Wonder. . . . And there we were. Right up there with them!

Gloria was determined to record a new song called "Anything for You," but in this case the producers weren't behind it. They felt as strongly against recording it as Gloria felt for recording it. I could feel her emotion and her commitment to the song. She completely won me over. Gloria really believed in this song, and she communicated that very powerfully. Since the co-producers weren't willing to record it, I had two new members, Jorge Casas and Clay Oswald, to produce it. The song was a monster hit, reaching number one on the Billboard charts.

That wasn't an easy battle; few battles are. But it was worth waging. The stories of those early hits are really instructive, and I think of them often. I had to be persistent, respectful, communicative, and resourceful in order to get others to see what I was seeing.

By the late 1980s, we wanted to change Gloria's image along with how she was evolving and changing as a woman and an artist. Tommy Mottola, the new president of Sony (it had acquired CBS), took a personal interest in Gloria's career and was very supportive of what we wanted to do. As soon as Tommy and I met, we clicked personally and professionally. Tommy had been in the music business since he was a kid, first as a performer himself, then as a manager, and later working in music publishing as well. He knew the business inside and out and backward, and was a keen spotter of hot trends. He had great faith in the Latin market but not the knowledge he figured he needed.

Tommy and I got along like a house on fire and have been very close friends now for over twenty years. I consider him another brother—if he's shopping and spots something he likes for me, like a tie, he'll often pick it up. I introduced him to a young Mexican singer I was producing, and he and Thalia eventually married and now have a young daughter. Tommy's support and enthusiasm have been invaluable. He was the key guy in the company to get everyone excited about something.

Even though she was a mother and a wife, Gloria was still quite young and certainly plenty sexy! Gloria changed her makeup and hair-style and hired a personal trainer. In the music business, image is as important as sound. It was also important for us not to perpetuate stereotypes. Gloria's look was elegant and classy, like her. The new image accompanied the next step in Gloria's evolution as an artist: She launched her first solo album, *Cuts Both Ways*. Gloria had not only grown as a singer, performer, and recording artist; she was now a full-fledged song-writer. She wrote seven and cowrote two more of the album's twelve tracks. *Cuts Both Ways* was her biggest album and established her as an important songwriter in the United States.

Gloria had been writing and collaborating for years, but during the *Let It Loose* tour, when Nayib and I were not able to be with her all the time, she usually went back to her hotel room after a concert and, just as she did as a child, found solace in her guitar. She became quite prolific during that period, and she continues to write a lot. Gloria's hard work paid off. In 1989 Gloria and the Miami Sound Machine were named "Favorite Pop/Rock Band/Duo/Group" at the American Music Awards (following Bon Jovi!). The same year, BMI (Broadcast Music, Inc., the prestigious international music agency) named Gloria Pop Songwriter of the Year (I received the BMI Latin songwriter award myself in 2005). Not only was she the first Latina given that honor; she was also the first woman.

I was so proud of my wife.

I FELT—AND STILL FEEL—VERY STRONGLY that you can't let others decide your destiny. If I was going to fail, it was going to be at something I believed in. I also knew and still know that there is a great deal of merit in trying, and, if it happens, a lot to be learned from failing. It's better to fail with your own idea. At least you tried it out, and maybe you can do it again and succeed.

I'm not going to pretend that I didn't have moments of self-doubt or worry. Sure I did. There was a lot on the line in those early days for me:

my good name, my job, my future. And the same was true for all the people working with us. They had made plenty of sacrifices for their music, and I felt very much responsible for all of them too.

In looking back now, I almost (almost!) think those early battles were the easy ones. When you're young and full of energy (and supremely self-confident, as so many young people are) you're in the right place and frame of mind to create and to conquer. You feel like there's nothing you can't do. The paradox of success is that with each victory the stakes get higher. As you take on new challenges, even though you have a track record, everyone is watching you. Some people want you to succeed. And some really do want you to fail.

I'm a creative person. Every single day I feel a need to create something new. As much as I loved writing and recording, I always knew there were plenty of other things I could try my hand at. And that's precisely why the stakes get higher. Yes, I was a successful songwriter and musician, but that didn't necessarily mean, in the eyes of many, that I could also be a producer or anything else I would later try my hand at.

A solid track record—not just of results but also of professional conduct (meeting deadlines, budgets)—will go a long way toward convincing people that you can try something else, but more than anything, you first have to believe in yourself. You can conquer the internal issue if you really want to, because those are the ones most under your control.

To recap, the most common internal issues are your own negative thinking, failure to prepare, self-doubt. They can be conquered by a belief in yourself, preparedness, and persistence. You need to identify these self-inflicted problems before you take on the external ones, the ones farthest from your control.

Once you've identified, dealt with, and overcome the internal problems, you're ready to face others. To turn no into yes, remember, you first have to say yes to yourself.

CHAPTER TWENTY-ONE

Embrace New Markets

The Latino market is now the fastest growing in the country. In 2009 the Census Bureau reported that there are almost forty-seven million Hispanics in the United States, about one in six of the population. They predict there will be sixty million Hispanics in the United States by 2020. Latinos have more kids than the average, so the ratio will keep going up: In 2008 we made up 14 percent of the population but accounted for almost 25 percent of the births. And we're younger. The median age of Latinos is twenty-eight versus about thirty-seven for the whole population.

Just think about the opportunities there. Latinos are invigorating the economy in the United States. We're adding people, reversing what would otherwise be a drop in total population. On average we're younger, so it's a dynamic group. There is so much interest, and acceptance, of almost all things Latin: our food, our music, and our literature. This is only the beginning of all we can do.

What a different landscape it is from when I arrived in 1968. Latinos need to learn how to take advantage of what is already here. In terms of media, the scene is now set. There are major players in all areas: two major Spanish-language national networks (the independently owned Univision, and NBC-owned Telemundo), as well as a host of local Spanish-language channels in heavily Hispanic areas. Spanish-language radio is the fastest growing in the country; and in print media numerous brands now have sister publications of major English-language publications. I'm one of the few people who has established working relationships with both Telemundo and Univision, doing the show *Frecuencia* on Telemundo for three years and the Nuestra Navidad specials for Univision (sponsored by Target).

Latinos have become an important group of consumers as our numbers have increased. Latinos today are better positioned than ever, in part because of our numbers and also because of our education. And corporate America has woken up to that reality. There is a lot more outreach and a lot more awareness of Latinos. Just look at all the advertising and marketing campaigns directed at us in Spanish and in English. It makes sense—if you're in position to market to American consumers you have to take account of the Hispanic market and embrace it. Think about it: There are more Hispanics in the United States (47 million) than there are people in Spain (population 40 million).

We have been able to parlay our experience in the market into expertise and have been able to make a positive contribution. We've done consulting work for, had partnerships with, and created campaigns for a number of major U.S. corporations, such as Sprint, AT&T, and Target. Now more than ever U.S. institutions are looking for qualified Latino talent. Banks and other financial institutions now actively and aggressively seek out Latino clients. And Latinos have responded by being ready for the opportunities that are presented to us. Imagine speaking English and Spanish well, as so many people do, knowing how this country and other countries operate, what the norms and rules are for doing business here and elsewhere. Those are all great advantages. This generation coming up is very impressive and well positioned to take advantage.

Nevertheless, there is a great need in our community for mentoring of this generation. The high school dropout rate among Latinos, especially in urban centers, is the highest in the country, and growing. As the Latino community's numbers increase, the community needs to take a greater leadership role. Our leaders won't only be political leaders; they will need to be leaders in all walks of life. Our youth need role models, and I feel a great responsibility to encourage and mentor the people I work with directly. As someone in the entertainment field and a public figure myself, I have the additional responsibility of encouraging my colleagues to be role models themselves and to mentor others in turn. For the community to grow and prosper, we urgently need mentoring and leadership in all areas.

I've long been involved in the careers of young Latino performers like Ricky Martin, Alejandro Fernández, Thalia, and Shakira. But they were already known and experienced when I began to work with them. There are so many unknown raw talents out there.

One way to create the new sounds the music industry craves is to fuse different traditions and to link up with people of other cultures and with other talents. A few years back, I briefly joined forces with Sean "P. Diddy" Combs. He invited me to create a new label with him, an offshoot of his Bad Boy label called Bad Boy Latino.

Sean is an amazing guy, multitalented, cutting-edge, counterintuitive, and very hardworking. He not only spots trends way before others do; he creates trends. Sean has been very successful as an artist, a producer of other artists, and an actor, and he had branched out into other businesses as well. You probably know his very popular Sean John clothing line, right? We were certainly kindred spirits with a lot in common. It seemed like a good fit. Our partnership no longer exists, but I tell this story to illustrate the opportunities that exist in other markets.

Besides Sean's obvious respect for and admiration of Latino talent— which I appreciated—he is also a sharp businessman, and he shared my concerns about the slow pace of change in the music industry. Companies in the industry, as in many industries, were becoming megaconglomerates, something that makes it harder and harder to maintain the more intimate working relationships with artists. We wanted to create not only the sounds that would appeal to listeners; we wanted to make those sounds available to them in the way that, more and more, listeners are accessing them.

So we entered into a sponsorship alliance with Sprint, the wireless company. They were the first wireless company to make live streaming video available on cell phones (and also the first to make Latino-themed content available on cell phones). Getting content via cell phone isn't only the future; it's the here and now.

Bad Boy Latino was more than just a cross-ethnic business partnership, although that is really important and pretty unique. Not only is there a lot of opportunity for crossover between African-American and Latino artists; audiences in both communities are among this country's biggest, if not the biggest, trendsetters.

I KNEW I WANTED TO be educated and to learn as much as I could. One of the many things I've been told I couldn't do was learn music. Back in the seventies I went to a high school in Miami and asked if I could take classes to formally learn music. They said no, I was too old. They said I should have been learning music when I was eleven. When I was eleven there were a lot of other things going on in my life. Well, this over-the-hill nonmusician went on to get about fifty Grammy nominations. Much later, when I was established in my career, I had an idea to help Hispanic music in this country by setting up a separate Grammy ceremony specifically dedicated to Latino music. It was something else I was told would never happen. But it was my fondest dream to have a telecast to showcase our diversity. I really wanted to honor and pay homage to all the greats, those who had blazed trails, like Carlos Santana and José Feliciano and so many others.

As I've said throughout this book, new sounds, new looks, new ideas, and new talents go against the grain, and you need to constantly be selling them. In this area, one of the contributions I am most proud of is the Latin Grammys. And getting that to fruition took ten years of hard sell, but the success of the Latin Grammys was—unfortunately—met with what I consider a lot of skepticism in the form of criticism.

Even within the Latino community, people questioned why we needed a separate awards ceremony for Latino music. To me, and to most music lovers, the answer was pretty obvious. The label "Latino music" was a one-size-fits-all category. And Latino music is so much more varied than just tropical or *norteño* or rock *en español*, etc. We needed a separate recognition for our music, because it was not being fully recognized in the mainstream, and neither were our artists and engineers.

It was easy to see the influence that Latin music was having within the United States and far beyond our borders.

As more and more Latinos were selling more and more records, and many were also crossing over and getting airplay on general market radio, it seemed like a huge oversight not to recognize those artists and their music. Although there were separate categories of Latin music at the Grammys, too many artists were competing for too few awards. And it was time for additional recognition from their peers.

Remember Ricky Martin's appearance at the Grammys in 1999 singing "La Copa de la Vida"? It electrified the show! Ricky was a huge star in Spanish and was about to cross over into English. I had persuaded Mike Greene, the president of the National Academy of Recording Arts and Sciences (NARAS), to put Ricky front and center during that telecast. And sure enough, that was the performance that got everyone excited. And it certainly gave a boost to our case for separate Latin Grammys.

The Grammys are more than just an award and a glamorous show. They help create greater awareness of who is doing what in terms of music, and I don't just mean they are a marketing event. They really let music lovers know what's out there, and for musicians and producers it is important peer recognition. In the case of the Latin Grammys, we wanted to do the same.

In 1997, NARAS launched its first international venture, the Latin Recording Academy. An important difference between the Grammys and the Latin Grammys is that the Latin Grammys encompass the entire Spanish-speaking and Portuguese-speaking world. So the voting membership is international and U.S.-based, just as our artists are. Winners come from Brazil, Mexico, Colombia, Spain, and so on. The process to choose Latin Grammy winners is the same as that for the Grammys—one vote per member.

With the support of NARAS, we were finally able to launch the Latin Grammys and the award show in 2000. The show made history when it was broadcast from the Staples Center in Los Angeles on September 13, 2000—it was the first time a Spanish-language show was broadcast on network TV, on CBS, in prime time. (Most presenters spoke in English, but all performances were in Spanish or Portuguese.)

I had been such a driving force behind getting the Latin Grammys launched that some people criticized me and the awards ceremony, calling it "Emilio's show." There are always those who want to rain on your parade, though, so you can't let it get to you. But in this case it bothered me. This was long-sought-after recognition for our people, and yet even Latinos within the industry were critical. This wasn't about me. It was about the efforts and talents of so many people, after so many years. It was a very important step forward.

Only two days before the inaugural Latin Grammys, on September 11, 2000, the Latin Academy of Recording Arts and Sciences (LARAS) honored me as its first Person of the Year. The award was given to me at a dinner in Beverly Hills. The dinner was a fund-raiser for MusiCares, a charity for musicians who are experiencing financial, medical, or personal difficulties. The dinner included a tribute organized by Phil Ramone (in his amazing career he has produced, among many others, Tony Bennett, Bob Dylan, Barbra Streisand, Paul Simon, Billy Joel . . . and Gloria!). Gloria, Shakira, Carlos Vives, Juan Luis Guerra, and José Feliciano were among those who performed during the tribute. I didn't seek the recognition and I didn't expect it, but I was deeply touched by it. By that time, I had already won seven Grammys (and been nominated for another sixteen or so), but this recognition really went straight to my heart.

The following year, the Latin Grammys show was scheduled to be held again in Los Angeles on September 11. Because of the tragic events earlier that same day, the show was canceled. Awards were given out on October 31, 2001, during a press conference in Los Angeles.

Both the Latin Grammys and LARAS have only grown in importance and are becoming very influential. The Latin Grammys have also been held in New York, Miami, Houston, and Las Vegas. Cities around the country have expressed interest in hosting the event. It has become a big draw and brings in a lot of revenue to a city—who wouldn't want it?

When I see this generation of musicians receiving their awards, it only reinforces my belief that you have to remain faithful to yourself and not be bothered by what other people think. What is important is to stick to it, to listen to your heart, and to believe in yourself and your ideas.

When I started out so many years ago, the Hispanic community didn't exist as a separate market. What other markets are on the horizon? What other groups and communities are out there that we haven't discovered or even addressed yet?

CHAPTER TWENTY-TWO

Take Care of Business

Making it in the music business is about a lot more than putting out hit records. Believe me, there are countless singers and bands who have been great at the music part of the music business but absolutely lousy at the business end. In many cases it wasn't their fault, or, at least, their failings were understandable. Young bands have signed bad contracts since the dawn of time. They've been so anxious to get a deal that they've signed their lives away. Many flounder without legal, business, and professional creative help. I stepped back from the performing side of music a long time ago, and a significant part of my life has involved taking care of business like this.

To make money out of music—as in any business where you create the product—you really have to have a hand in as much of your own work as possible. It's not just about the marketing aspect we talked about before. When you're an artist and you work with others, your success, especially the financial aspect, is shared. The music business is so much more than singing and making records. There are concerts, appearances, videos, publishing, and songwriting, just to name a few other areas.

Songwriting is an important part of our music business, and the publishing aspect accounts for the lion's share of music revenues. A hit record is very rewarding for an artist, but it is even more rewarding, in terms of dollars in the bank, for the songwriter. So the best of all possible worlds is for you to write your own songs and own the rights to them too. From the beginning we performed our own material. When you start out, you usually have to perform covers of familiar favorites just to please the crowd. But as you gain a following, more and more people are going to want to hear your original material. We always managed to do both, since we performed in English and Spanish.

I cannot emphasize enough how important it is to have control of material that you create. I think this is something artists are keenly aware of. But so many artists do not have a business sense, or even a sense of self-preservation. If you create something, anything, don't you want credit for it? If you want to be able to continue to create, to have the time to dedicate to your craft and not have to work at something else to pay the bills, you are going to want that credit to translate into cash. You need to be paid for the work you do. And in the case of songs, when someone plays them, when someone sings them, and even when someone adapts them for commercial purposes, you are entitled to get paid— but only if you own the song, and only if that is clearly established. You should retain the rights to your songs as long as you have the infrastructure to license and collect royalties.

Back when we started out in the 1970s and we recorded our first albums, we lost the rights to our songs, and I knew that was a bad deal. Because of that, in 1979 we set up our own publishing company, Foreign Imported Productions and Publishing, and from then on we have owned and/or administered 100 percent of the copyright on all of the songs on which Gloria and/or I have songwriting credits. When we signed with Sony (then CBS) in the early 1980s, I also insisted that we retain the rights to our songs. I can tell you that that was perhaps the smartest move I ever made in business. (Earlier, we had lost the rights to a couple of albums. In time, I made sure to go back and reacquire those rights and the masters of the albums. We repackaged the songs as a greatest-hits album and sold millions of copies.)

Every time any one of our songs is played or licensed to be recorded or performed or for any use, we receive royalties. Careful records are kept throughout the industry, and payment is made on a biannual basis. For us, as music publishers and songwriters, this has always been an important revenue stream. In fact, the real money earner in the music business is not in recording or in performing; it's in songwriting and in retaining the rights to your songs. The industry standard is that the writer receives 50 percent of the royalties and the music publisher receives the other 50 percent. If the song is cowritten or copublished, the royalties are also divided up accordingly. For a songwriter, sharing the royalties is a good deal, since they are not paying any overhead. The music publisher is responsible for licensing and collecting, so part of the publisher's takings pay for overhead.

Our songwriters worked under the same terms, and for years that situation worked well for all involved. Songwriters who work for us on exclusive contract are paid a percentage of royalties. Many young songwriters were not only given the opportunity to work with more experienced writers; their songs were recorded by top artists and many, many of those songs became monster hits. Our songwriters have written number one hits for Gloria, Shakira, Jennifer Lopez, Ricky Martin, Marc Antony, Thalia, Alejandro Fernández, and many other artists.

Foreign Imported Productions and Publishing represents the rights to over two thousand songs by a number of different songwriters. That's a lot of songs to keep track of. The only way to make sure we're paid what we are due is to have people work full-time to administer this business. It is truly a business in and of itself. And a pretty complicated one at that. By 2003, the songwriting and publishing arm of Estefan Enterprises had grown so big that we entered into a deal with Universal Music Publishing Group to administer our catalog outside of North America.

BY THE EARLY 1990s, I had already started to produce other artists, and I was dedicating more and more of my time to studio work and less to touring. I had begun to work hard at developing new talent: songwriters, producers, recording artists. Since we had bought Crescent Moon

Studios in 1990, that had become one of the main focuses of my work—my "baby," if you will.

In 1994, together with Sony, we set up Crescent Moon Records, and at the same time I became president of music development for Sony Music Entertainment.

Jon Secada is a longtime collaborator and a very talented singer and songwriter. He toured with Gloria in the late 1980s and always did a spotlight song during her shows. We soon began collaborating on songs. After Gloria's accident, he cowrote the big hit "Coming out of the Dark," and after that we started work on his first solo album called *Jon Secada.* It was released in 1992 and had four top-thirty hits (four number ones in the *Billboard* Hot Latin charts), including "Just Another Day Without You," this time with Gloria singing backup for him.

Jon is a talented and prolific songwriter and we've enjoyed a long and fruitful partnership. He was one of many songwriter/producer/recording artists I have worked with over the years in relationships that for both sides have been mutually beneficial. We always had a great time working together. Jon was able to write several top hits in English and Spanish for a number of artists, including Ricky Martin and Jennifer Lopez, even coproducing for Jennifer.

I like spotting and nurturing young talent. I've been so fortunate, and had so many great mentors and role models myself along the way, that I've always been committed to giving back by grooming young musicians. I love being surrounded by talented people, especially ones I've developed personal relationships with, but when it's time for them to move on—almost always because they want to—they do so with my best wishes. What could be more satisfying than to see someone you've believed in believe in him- or herself and move on to bigger and better things?

In some cases, our real estate and hospitality businesses were complementary to each other, but one didn't always depend on the other. I have always run our music ventures in a more organic way, with one area feeding off of or depending on the other. My job as a producer—in twenty-five words or less—is to deliver recordings to a record company by a certain date, at a certain budget. There's actually a lot more to it than that, or at least in the way I do things, there is! As I see it, and as I've always done it, producing is the whole package. You manage the artist's studio time, and you find the music and musicians who will best suit that artist's taste, style, and genre.

You work closely with the artist, understanding his or her goals and vision, and you try to help the artist achieve that. Just as the artist can't do everything alone, neither can a producer. It is a very special collaborative relationship. The producer needs to understand the concept the artist wants, and needs to work with the artist to choose songs and musicians to create that sound. But experience has taught me that artists often get stuck in a rut, and because of their own internal pressures to create and maintain their own identity as artists and celebrities, they often run back to the tried and true. And their record companies want them to deliver "more of the same." If artists were better businesspeople, or tried to have a better understanding of the business at least, they would be in a better position to protect their own art.

This is going to sound contradictory, perhaps, but taking care of business doesn't mean dishing out more of the same. Quite the contrary. You have to grow as an artist, a businessperson, an entrepreneur, a craftsman. While you can't be an expert in everything—that's why we have and hire experts, to advise us—it is imperative that you have as organic an understanding of your chosen field as possible.

CHAPTER TWENTY-THREE

Think out of the Box

I think in all businesses there is a certain need to be counterintuitive. You often need to go against the conventional wisdom. If an artist always plays rock, why not try a ballad? If an artist sings in Spanish, why not try English or the other way around?

One example for me of being counterintuitive was the making of one of Gloria's most successful albums ever, *Mi Tierra*, which was released in 1993. Gloria and I have done over twenty albums together, and each one has been different. Our mainstream success with the Miami Sound Machine, and for Gloria as a solo artist, was achieved for many years singing in English. We had hit the big time by crossing over into English. But we always knew, at some point, that we wanted to go back and record an album in Spanish, again as a tribute to our heritage.

Why record *Mi Tierra*? It's quite simple: because we wanted to. Gloria and I move easily between our two cultures, but our Latin roots are sunk very, very deep, and the pull to sing in Spanish was strong. *Mi Tierra* was an honest project, something so close to us, so real, and so original. It was also a great example of thinking out of the box. And when you do projects like that, authentic and heartfelt, people respond.

We got together an amazing group of musical talent for the album. It was like a who's who of Latin stars: Cachao and Paquito D'Rivera; Arturo Sandoval and Nestor Torres . . . and also the London Symphony Orchestra string section!

The release of *Mi Tierra* caught people by surprise. First, it was unique, Gloria's first solo album entirely in Spanish. That alone got a lot of attention. And then the backdrop of the album was our own personal story: two kids who had left their country (*Mi Tierra*: *My Land*) but never, ever left their culture behind. We were at the top of the English charts, but we departed from the tried and true to sing in Spanish—*an idea born in the heart.* Just doing the album in Spanish was enough to make noise and generate interest. But there was opposition, of course. So many people asked us, "You're doing so well in English, why bother with Spanish?" It was an unusual move, and we took a chance by making that album. Yet another reverse crossover!

By 1993 we were in a position to take a risk. Sure, we did it from the position of security that we'd established with our success, but we were laying our reputations on the line, and we had a lot to lose if the album was a critical and commercial bomb. We thought big and took the chance, confident that what was right in our hearts would appeal to a lot of people. We got a lot of support for the venture. Tommy Mottola was right behind us. We were nominated for the title song, "Mi Tierra," so the president of NARAS, Mike Greene, had Gloria sing it on the Grammy awards show, which demonstrated how Gloria was busting through the genre limits that some people like to place on artists.

Mi Tierra blazed that particular trail. It sold millions of albums. In fact *Mi Tierra* was the first Latin album to sell more than a million copies. It held the number one spot on the charts for two years in the United States as the top tropical/salsa Latin album. Gloria won her first Grammy for this album after many nominations. And she felt particular pride and satisfaction that it was for work in Spanish. The response around the world was just as gratifying. It was a giant success in France, Germany, and Italy, and it still holds the record as the biggest-selling album of all time by an international artist in Spain. The record remains very dear to me and Gloria. Gloria got to sing the song "Mi Tierra" in Cuba when she performed it in a concert at the Guantánamo Bay base, which was a very emotional moment for her. Gloria said, "I don't want to cry here." But, of course, she teared up.

Without *Mi Tierra* other successes would likely not have happened.

We were at the forefront as a whole Latin movement crossed over internationally. The perfect example of that, and of how to plan a career, is our work with Shakira.

Shakira Mubarak was already a big star in her native Colombia and throughout Latin America by the time she came to see me in Miami to ask me to manage her career and help her break into the U.S. market. It was 1996, not long after Shakira had released her album *Pies Descalzos*, which was wildly successful in Colombia and Latin America.

She came to my office with Jairo Martinez, her manager. Shakira is even more charismatic in person than she is onstage—very, very bright, warm, an infectious smile—and she is very hardworking. Lots of great ideas . . . She is also a perfectionist, detail-oriented, passionate about her work, and very headstrong. She is also one of the most authentic artists I have ever met. That was as evident in our first meeting as it is today. She is always true to herself and what she wants.

And there was an instant chemistry between us. I liked her immediately. We clicked in an instant. We are both Lebanese, both coastal—she is from the Colombian Caribbean city Barranquilla—and both intensely and deeply devoted to family. It says a lot about her respect for her parents that Shakira—already successful and an astute businesswoman—brought them along to our subsequent meetings.

Shakira was barely twenty but had been performing since she was a little girl, first as an actress in Colombian soap operas and then as a singer. She wrote her first song when she was eight years old after an older half brother's death in a traffic accident. For years her father hid his grief behind dark glasses, so she called the song "Gafas Oscuras" ("Dark Glasses").

After an impromptu audition for a Sony Colombia music executive in a hotel lobby in Barranquilla when she was about thirteen, Shakira was signed to a three-record deal. Her first album was a moderate success, but she was not pleased with the production on the second album, so she did not agree to promote it. That's kind of an extraordinary stance for such a young artist, but pretty typical of Shakira. She is a perfectionist to the core.

Her third album, *Pies Descalzos* (*Barefoot*), was released in 1996, when she was eighteen. That album made her a major recording artist in the region, with sales of five million copies, one million in Brazil alone. By then, she had become a *rockera*, a guitar-wielding, leather-pants-wearing, hard-core *rockera*. And that was when we met. She was not a little girl or a starving artist. She wasn't looking for fame. She was looking for something different: quality.

While her big, versatile, and colorful voice is her trademark, Shakira is also really the whole package as an artist and performer. She can write, play guitar, dance, and has incredible stage presence. She is brilliant in every sense of the word. She shines. She is, however, such a perfectionist that she can often be surprisingly insecure. Artists are temperamental by nature; that's not a cliché. It's part of the creative personality. So they tend to require a lot of hand-holding. And in Shakira's case, her talent also matched her needs.

Shakira wasn't afraid of the U.S. market or performing in large venues, or even touring and doing media. But she was really reticent about singing and performing in English. Her knowledge of the language was almost nil, a little bit surprising for someone who had grown up on American rock and pop. From the outset I told her that if she wanted to break into the U.S. market, she would have to be prepared to also work in English.

"I don't know English," she said. "How can I do an album in English?"

"You will," I assured her.

I never told her to stop writing and performing in Spanish. *On the contrary*; I thought that was a key part of her identity, and I knew that her Spanish-language material would find an enormous and receptive audience in the United States and elsewhere.

We also talked that day about her image. She was very cute, almost innocent-looking, so the leather-pants *rockera* outfits were not really in keeping with her hair and makeup. She knew that, and she was prepared to change. She was not afraid to take risks; she was looking for change.

A major part of our plan of action was to get her to learn English, and to learn it well enough to not only be able to sing in English but to actually also be able to write in English.

Next, we needed get to work on an album. I was by now the head of Sony Worldwide Artist Development and I felt strongly that she needed a new contract, so we negotiated a contract with Sony Worldwide. It might have been better for me to sign her to Crescent Moon, my label, but, because I was her manager, for her and her career, I helped her get the best possible deal.

So we had a huge project ahead of us, one that only the whole company, Estefan Enterprises, could take on, really. Shakira's potential was so obvious to me, but tapping that potential was also going to be an enormous undertaking.

We agreed to work together, and Shakira agreed to move to Miami from Colombia. That was a key part of the strategy. She had to be here to work with us. We hired a private English tutor for her, got her a personal trainer, and she and I set to work planning her next album.

When we became her management company, managing Shakira was a small part of our portfolio, and although helping her break into the U.S. market was an important goal for me, I didn't see it as an all-consuming activity. By the end of the three years and three albums we did together, Shakira had begun to take up far too much of our time. And I say that not because she wasn't worthy of our time; but managing another artist besides Gloria was not part of our core business. We had managed other artists—Carlos Ponce, Jon Secada—but combined they did not represent the commercial success that Shakira did. And, again, that amount of . . . call it what you will—success, ambition, talent—has to be met with an equal measure of dedication from management.

The first album I produced for Shakira was entirely in Spanish, *Dónde Están los Ladrones?* (*Where Are the Thieves?*). Eight of the eleven tracks on the album became singles, perhaps the most famous being "Ojos Así" ("Eyes Like Yours"). I thought she should reference her Arabic roots and move away a bit from just the pure pop and rock *en español* sound. That song really set her apart and showed not only her vocal range but, in the song's video, Shakira displays her considerable belly-dancing talents. (She told me she had been belly dancing since she was four years old, since her father first took her to a Lebanese restaurant, and then she later took dance lessons.)

Dónde Están los Ladrones? was a major commercial success, selling one million copies in the United States and more than eight million worldwide. It hit number one in Argentina, Mexico, Spain, and, of course, Colombia. It was *Billboard*'s top Latin album and made it to 131 on *Billboard*'s top two hundred—not bad at all for an album entirely in Spanish.

Not only the quality of her work but the publicity blitz we unleashed worked phenomenally well. Shakira made the covers of *TIME* and *Newsweek*—what could be more representative of the U.S. general market?—and she still had not released songs in English. Her next album, an MTV Unplugged, included almost all the songs from *Dónde Están los Ladrones?* The record company discouraged us from selling the Unplugged version. Shakira even received phone calls from people high up in the company discouraging her. She told me about the calls, and I told those people not to call my artist behind my back.

Our long-term relationship with Pepsi also benefited Shakira. I suggested they listen to Shakira and sign her for both markets..

She released four songs for Pepsi commercials, and they sponsored her Tour Anfibio, an extensive tour of the United States and Latin America, to support both *Dónde Están los Ladrones?* and MTV Unplugged. I was anxious for her to record in English but she still wasn't ready. When she came back from the tour, we began work in earnest on her first English-language album.

Her English was coming along phenomenally well. Shakira still had an accent, but she had become very comfortable even doing interviews in English. Yet she was still nervous about singing and recording in English. Gloria was a tremendous help in that regard. Initially, Shakira wrote her songs entirely in Spanish and then Gloria would translate them into English. But Gloria would also literally go into the studio with Shakira while Shakira recorded in English. Shakira wanted and needed that level of reassurance that she was doing a good job. (I said she was a perfectionist.)

Despite our track record, both with Shakira and with other artists, Tommy Mottola was resistant to launching her as a crossover artist. He was afraid that she was getting established in the Latino market and he didn't want her to lose traction there. But we knew that this was the right move, that more than ever there was an audience ripe for Shakira, and that she was ripe for them. Gloria, who had worked so closely with Shakira and had mentored and nurtured her talent, was particularly fierce in her defense of Shakira. She and Tommy got into a big blowout argument over Shakira. Gloria was not going to back down and neither was I.

And Tommy was a key player in this plan. We really needed to convince him—he was the gear to get the company behind her. (Fortunately, he is a really good listener.)

Laundry Service, Shakira's first English album, came out in late 2001. We had worked on it for well over a year. Initially, Shakira was going to translate some of the hits from *Dónde Están los Ladrones?* and include them on the new album, but she decided against that in the end. She felt strongly about doing original material for this new venture, as risky as it was.

Shakira had her critics; that's for sure. When the album came out some of the most prominent critics in the business said the writing was weak and that Shakira was "lost in translation." It's a good thing audiences make up their own minds, though. *Laundry Service* debuted at number three on the *Billboard* 200 and was soon certified triple platinum in the United States (with sales of more than three million copies). It wound up becoming one of the biggest-selling albums of 2002. A Spanish-language version, *Servicio de Lavanderia*, was later released in Latin America and met with similar success. The album has sold over thirteen million copies worldwide. It was a great time for her and for me.

The success of *Laundry Service* made her more in demand than ever, almost more than we could have predicted. There was no single incident that led to the end of our managerial relationship with Shakira. We still got along personally and professionally phenomenally well. But we did not want to continue to dedicate so many resources to just one artist. There were other projects I wanted to do and other projects we wanted to undertake as a company. As Shakira's popularity grew, so did demands on her time, and in turn, so did demands on our time. When you manage an artist, that person wants—and deserves—your full attention, and that pretty much means that you have to be with that artist whenever and wherever he or she is working.

In Shakira's case, she was traveling all over the world almost nonstop, and that would have meant that I was away all the time. If I am in Miami, I can also do other work—produce other artists, etc.—but just being away from my home base meant I couldn't attend to my other businesses.

We had a very cordial parting of the ways, so cordial that we even helped Shakira find her new management team, who are managing her to this date. Shakira is the highest-selling Colombian artist of all time, having sold more than fifty million albums worldwide, with two Grammys, eight Latin Grammys, and fifteen *Billboard* awards under her belt. Shakira has blossomed into the consummate artist and public figure. She is gracious and continues to be extraordinarily hardworking, not just as an artist but as the head of a foundation, the Pies Descalzos Foundation, which helps underprivileged children. She is an exemplary philanthropist, not just in Latin America but in the international arena.

Shakira is a marvelous role model not just for other Latino artists, but for young Latinos and young people in general.

For me, her success in the general market, the Latino market in the U.S., and worldwide have given me great pride as a manager, producer, and businessman. The success of that plan is the perfect example not only of many things coming together at once, but also of vision and good planning. And, of course, of building upon past successes, and of having blazed a trail for other Latino artists.

Perhaps the nicest part of being a part of her success, though, was a very sweet letter I received from her father, which thanked me, saying he could die in peace, knowing his daughter was in good hands. As a father, I can tell you, there is no greater compliment than that.

YOU MIGHT MAKE GREAT MUSIC, but people have to be made aware that that music exists. Releasing a record is kind of like a tree falling in a forest—if there is no one around, no one will hear it. It won't make a sound. You have to make sure music gets heard. And when you do something against the grain, you have to make an extra effort to make sure people know that you are doing something special, something that you believe in. That's where marketing plays a huge role. I make no apologies for returning to this theme. There's nothing more important in the process. Other aspects might have equal importance—creating your sound, writing a song—but nothing is *more* important.

I love marketing. I have since I got to see what it was when I started at Bacardi. But I don't define it as a narrow campaign strategy. It really is about getting people's attention, getting them to listen, and keeping them intrigued—the end product will, or won't, hold their interest. You have to put it in front of them first and give them an opportunity to like it. You need to organize every element of a marketing plan so carefully. Every market is unique in terms of taste; you can't be everywhere at once, and yet timing is critical. Your goal is to get your product to as many people as possible.

In our first deal with Sony the label had a marketing budget. I went out and spent our own money over and above that; I knew how important it was that we didn't blow this chance. Now, when labels' marketing budgets are much smaller, we have to be creative. We've worked with great companies like AT&T and Starbucks with Gloria, increasing her exposure in partnership with enterprises that have great presence in their own markets.

In the case of an artist like Gloria, whose career I also manage, the "whole package" involves every aspect of marketing, from deciding the release date of the album; the cover shoot and other publicity shots;

whether or not you are going to tour, and when and where; press and media strategy; concerts, appearances, promotions.

Not just every industry but every product requires a different strategy. Some industries are going to be more capital-intensive. It's not cheap to market an album, for instance. At the same time, people waste money not being effective. In the case of an album, if you repeat yourself with a launch party, for instance, no matter how hip or glamorous the venue, you're not going to get much attention. It will look like "same old, same old"—and people may even think you are just promoting something old. Since the campaign is stale, the product may be too.

Changes and innovations are fantastic, and I couldn't be more excited about the way technology is improving our lives. But if not for marketing, we wouldn't even know about those innovations or why they are so wonderful. Marketing isn't about throwing lots of money around. It's about getting people's attention. There is so much going on around us all the time. Getting someone's attention and getting a message to stick in the information age is a big challenge. And if you are at all resourceful and creative, it's the kind of challenge that you welcome.

Ask yourself some key questions about your industry in order to figure out a marketing strategy or plan: Whom are you targeting? Whom is your product for? How are people accessing or buying the product? How are they going to know about it? I'm not giving you any trade secrets by telling you that in many ways the music industry has not caught up with the times. It is limping behind. How are people buying music? By downloading, by file sharing. The industry is losing money and not serving its customers by not paying attention to how they are buying music. The music industry is pretty sensitive to change and it should be leading the charge in marketing and sales. But it is a troubled industry right now.

You can have the best product or service, be it an album, a store, or a gas station, but if you don't market it somehow, it won't go anywhere. Quality alone will not be enough. (That said, quality is one of your strongest weapons in marketing. Don't waste your time even thinking about how to market something substandard.) Big corporations can spend the cash to get people's attention. But if you are small, you'd better be brilliant, resourceful, creative, and out of the box.

Every time we went into a new area, there was a learning curve. We were always able to apply some of what we knew from other businesses, but there really was one thing that we had clear from the start, and that is that running a business means growing a business. Whenever you go into a new area, it means you are looking for growth. Starting your own business and growing your business are all about enjoying your life and living it to the fullest. They are also about survival.

If you've started a company thinking that you are going to stay small and that it's good to be static, you are doomed to failure. Why? Because running a business is all about being open to new opportunities. You need to always have your eyes on taking your business to the next level. The only way for a business to survive is for that business to thrive. I don't mean that every small retailer has to want to be Target or Wal-Mart, or that restaurants have to become franchises as a measure of success. Always be on the lookout for how to grow the business by being open to new ideas and new people. Why? Because all businesses are about people—the people who work for you and the people who buy your product.

And when it comes to your product, you need to cultivate and grow your own inspiration.

CHAPTER TWENTY-FOUR

Get Inspired!

I t's time to backtrack and pick up where we left our discussion of motivation and inspiration. I've proved that I was motivated to succeed; how about the bigger picture of inspiration? If motivation gets your body in gear, inspiration is what nourishes and fills your soul. Everything comes into play here—your good work habits, your positive outlook, and your motivation will allow you to be more receptive to your own thoughts and feelings. Discipline (planning, punctuality, commitment, persistence) will also allow you the time and energy to come up with ideas. And that is essentially what inspiration is: the ideas that set you apart, that make you unique, that allow you to truly make your mark on the world.

Ideas are the coin of the realm in business. They are an almost incalculable asset. Ideas are so important that before we implement them, or even try to, we often patent or copyright them. In business, ideas are not just for products but also for services, for staffing, for resources, and ultimately for marketing and promotion—for getting the word out there about your great idea.

If you are an entrepreneur, you are in the ideas business. That is your stock in trade: a great idea. How do you come up with ideas? How do you recognize a good one when you see it, think it, feel it, imagine it, or dream it? What inspires a great idea?

There are three key facets to getting inspired. The first is imagination—be resourceful. Where are ideas needed and just what is a good idea? Allow yourself to think infinitely, without boundaries. The second? Listen to you heart—doing what you love will put you in the right place. And third, trust your intuition—believe in yourself. The last one is the most important of all. Why? Because if you don't trust yourself and have faith in your ideas, they will remain just that: ideas. You need faith to be able to act upon those ideas.

When I believe something, you can't change my mind. I think people should go with their intuition. The minute you start questioning most people they get insecure. I don't get insecure; I just get more entrenched in my belief. I can't tell you how many times I've had a strong instinct about something. It can come be a premonition. I remember when I bought on Star Island. I paid $600,000 for it and people thought I was crazy. All that money for a plot on an island? I bought two in the end, one for Gloria and me and one for my parents. I knew it was a great deal—I should have bought more, because now they go for over $20 million. When you have a strong feeling like that, and you have a track record, don't listen to anyone else.

As unromantic as it sounds, there actually is a process to getting inspired. Sure, there are lightning bolts, ideas that come in your dreams or ideas that pop into your head out of the blue. You can't force ideas. They do just come. The process is in being aware of those ideas, encouraging them, and nurturing them—and being fearless about exploring them.

You can't always schedule a time just to sit down and think about ideas. The creative process does simply happen, and it happens because you are excited about what you are doing. Ideas are born in the heart. You aren't likely to come up with a great idea about something you don't love or feel passionate about.

Your most valuable asset is yourself. So trust yourself and your intuition. You need to get in touch with those feelings and not be afraid to follow up and follow through on what you feel about a person, a place, or an idea. You are the best judge of what is best for you and what you are going to love.

Ideas come whether we are prepared for them or not. Even when we are asleep our minds are working and ideas come to us. (What do you think dreams are, after all?) Ideas are always around us and coming to us. It's important to be aware of that. Sometimes when you are about to fall asleep, an idea might pop into your head. Or you might wake up in the middle of the night with an idea. You need to learn to let those ideas come.

There are times when you'll have the luxury of just sitting and thinking, trying to come up with solutions or trying to invent something brand-new. Most of the time, though, you will be busy with your life and obligations. Ideas don't hit you only when you are relaxing, lying on a beach, or just hanging out. In fact, you will often find that in times of stress or great difficulties you get some of your best ideas. Why is that? I think sometimes ideas come to comfort us. The imagination is one of the greatest escape routes there is.

At the same time you can drive yourself crazy trying to capture an idea. Ideas can slip and slide and fight you like a fish on the end of a line. You can't be obsessive about it. I'd always say if it took me more than two weeks to get a song down, then it wasn't happening. At some point, before it gets counterproductive, you have to stop and move on to the next idea.

Sometimes you need to get external noise out of your head and just listen to your own ideas. Clear your mind of all distractions. But if you are stressed out, thinking too hard about difficulties and obstacles and having to get something done, you are probably going to stall the process. Along with your daily life and all its joys and obligations, being an entrepreneur requires you to find time where others can't. It requires you to find energy when you figure you've used up all that you have. That's why it's important to live an organized life, keep things in their place (that doesn't just mean hanging up your jacket—it also means doing things on time) so that you aren't distracted and you can be in touch with what is going on in your head and your heart.

The only way you can clear your mind of distractions is to take care of all your obligations. You give yourself more room to be inspired when you organize and respect your time. It might sound unexciting, but if you are already in the habit of taking care of business, you'll have more time and more energy to be aware of those flashes of lightning.

One way to get into the habit of hearing and feeling your own ideas is to pick a time just to think. I am most inspired in the mornings when I get up and it's quiet. When there are no distractions. I love the morning time, because that's when everything begins. The sun is coming up, and seeing the light gives me hope. I am well rested and my mind is clear.

An idea will hit me at almost any time, but I feel more positive energy in the morning. You might feel better at a different time of the day, but morning works best for me. You need to find your own best time. It might take a bit of tinkering to find those few minutes in the day when you can just listen to yourself, but it is well worth the effort.

Then get used to listening to your ideas. You might feel silly at first, just sitting trying to get inspired. But it's a good way to start. It's almost like an exercise, a relaxation exercise where you just listen to the sound of your breathing. In this case, you are listening to the sound of your ideas flowing. Get used to it. Listen. Listen to yourself and you will also get into the habit of listening well to others and to their ideas. But first, learn to listen to yourself.

Then think infinitely. In the privacy of your own mind, nothing is out of reach. So start to get comfortable with even the most outlandish ideas. Allow yourself a bit of time to get in touch with your ideas every day, and before you know it, you will be listening to your own ideas without even realizing it.

Believe in those ideas and have faith in them. If you like something, there is a reason for it. Others are just as likely to appreciate your idea if they see your passion for it. Be fearless in your enthusiasm for your dreams.

Imagine a completed idea. Writers often speak of the dread they feel when they see the blank page and nothing comes to mind. Musicians and other artists feel the same when they try to force the beginning of something. So my suggestion is not to force the beginning but to imagine the outcome.

A few years ago we bought a house in Vero Beach, several hours north of our home in Miami Beach. We wanted a getaway that we could drive to, and we wanted to go to an area that was relatively undeveloped for tourists.

Gloria and I found the perfect place, but you wouldn't have known it if you'd seen it when we did. It was old and run-down, and hadn't been occupied in a long time. But when I walked into the house, in my mind's eye I could see it refurbished, remodeled, and ready. I had a vision for the house, right down to the details. We purchased it right away and never looked back.

And you need to remember a good idea. You don't necessarily need to carry a notepad around everywhere you go—although that isn't a bad idea—but you do have to jot things down or you might lose those great ideas. I have developed design plans, planned marketing campaigns, and written song hooks on the spur of the moment. And lots of those were recorded on the backs of matchbooks, on gum wrappers, slips of paper, whatever was at hand.

But most of the time you are not going to have the luxury of sitting and thinking all day, nor is that necessarily conducive to all your best ideas. There is a lot to be said for noise, problems, and other external stimuli to get the creative juices and ideas flowing. You can't choose the time for when your best ideas will come to you. So remember, always be ready to be inspired.

Next step, be resourceful. Ideas will spring up right in front of you when you realize that you have so much to work with. We can do so much with so little, but we have also convinced ourselves that we need to spend, spend, and spend to be able to develop a successful project or idea. Not true. Some of the most charming and interesting ideas are built on established ideas or reused materials. So here's another mantra for you: recycle, renew, revive.

CHAPTER TWENTY-FIVE

Recycle, Renew, Revive

There are so many great things about our country and our culture, but one of the negatives about life in the United States is how we all take so much for granted. There is such an abundance here of food, of clothing, cars, money, furniture, electronics, and on and on. We have convinced ourselves that material goods like these are infinitely available. But they aren't. Raw materials, and by extension the goods we make from them, are finite.

Drive around any big city in the U.S. and just take a look at all the decent furniture left in Dumpsters or on the curb. It has become so expensive to renovate furniture—or has it become so cheap to buy?—that there's an epidemic of waste. Our wastefulness isn't just confined to furniture, of course. Portions of food in restaurants are excessive. Many restaurants simply toss out leftover food. People who have gone through what I did as a refugee or immigrant have a different attitude toward waste. It's in our nature to turn all the lights off in the house. We don't throw out things that somebody else needs or could use. We don't leave the faucet on when we brush our teeth. Being an immigrant, or anyone who has had to work hard to get anywhere, makes you think about not wasting resources and about being prudent.

It is hard to see so much waste, especially when you know there is so much need. If we get into the habit of recycling and using only what we need—and preserving the rest or giving it to someone who needs it—we would be so much more aware of the abundance we have.

As a society and as individuals we need to reeducate ourselves about how much we have. And what we can do with what we have, even if it does not seem like a lot. I love finding creative uses for things that most people would cast off as junk. It's more than a game or an outlet for my creativity. It is part of the way I look at things—I don't believe in wasting or spending money for the sake of spending money.

It's amazing how much you can do with so little, and for so little money. Ideas abound when you try to think up ways to reach the same result for less money. When I was working in the marketing department at Bacardi we were rolling out a national campaign for Bacardi rum cakes. The idea was to promote the cakes in supermarkets using beautiful young women who would display the cakes wearing sashes that said, MISS BACARDI RUM CAKE. The satin sashes we planned to use cost $30 each, which struck me as expensive, excessive even. And Bacardi needed hundreds of them.

Those sashes, although they were pretty, looked simple to make. I had an idea. It wasn't even a new idea—I'd done it before with the T-shirts I had made soon after I started with the company. I asked my boss if I could look into getting the sashes made for less money and sell them back to Bacardi. He agreed. A friend of mine worked at a funeral parlor hand-painting the ribbons that are displayed on wreaths and the backs of hearses. I went to see her to ask her how much they cost to make. She said they cost about $1.50 each. We made a deal. She would paint the sashes for me at night after work, and sell them to me for $7 each. I sold them to Bacardi for $15. Bacardi would be paying half of what they were paying, and I wound up making about $5,000 on the deal—just from being resourceful and thinking about excess and wastefulness.

Recycling is another part of being resourceful. I know a lot of people think that something made from recycled material is inferior, but I don't agree. Consider a table made of an old window or door compared to something new bought from an upscale furniture shop. I think an old window transformed into a tabletop can be charming and full of history. That's not to say that a chic and sleek new table couldn't be gorgeous, but the old window would have its own story and could be beautiful in its own right to boot.

Once when I was browsing in an antiques shop I came across some beautiful silver plates. From the intricate patterns etched on them I figured the plates were North African, and it turned out they were from Morocco. As I looked them over I began to imagine the silver plates not hung up on a wall but on a table, a dark wood table. The more I thought about them, the more I saw the plates not set *on* the dark wood table, but *in* the dark wood table.

I bought the plates and went home and drew a design with the plates incorporated in the tabletop. Then I had a carpenter build one long, high table and three smaller tables. Next time you are in Miami Beach, drop by the Cardozo Bar and Grill in our Cardozo Hotel. There they are. And the canoes that we used in Gloria's video for "Wrapped," which we filmed in the Peruvian highlands, have become part of the bar at our Bongos Cuban Café in Miami. I just thought the canoes were too nice to leave behind.

Recycling is important in the creative process. I don't mean copying—I mean taking something, items, ideas—and using it more fully. It's very satisfying to take something and give it new life, be it a jacket, a frame, a table, a plate of leftover food, a beloved rhythm or sound. This isn't about being cheap; it's about being creative and resourceful. Resources are finite and we have to use them well. Creative people like the challenge of recycling. And something new built on or out of something old has a certain positive energy.

Revival—giving new life to something—is another way of being resourceful. One of the best examples of this, and one that is closest to my heart, is the music of a beloved Cuban musician, Israel López, better known as Cachao. Called the Godfather of Mambo, Cachao had an enormous influence on Cuban music for decades, beginning with his creation of mambo in the thirties. Cachao, a bassist, and his brother, Orestes, who played several instruments, wrote thousands of songs together, but after the revolution, Cachao was virtually silenced.

Cachao followed a similar route to my own—he left Cuba for Spain in 1962, and spent a couple of years in Europe before immigrating to the United States. He finally came to Miami in the 1980s in order to live out his remaining years in peace. The actor Andy Garcia heard that Cachao was living in Miami and playing in restaurants, and Andy approached me about recording Cachao's music, so that it wouldn't be lost forever.

We'd just started Crescent Moon Records and I wanted to sign Cachao. I called Tommy Mottola, and said I'd just signed my first artist. Tommy said, "Is he good-looking?" and I said, "Well, sort of." Tommy said, "Does he sing well?" and I said, "No." Then Tommy said, "Well, does he tour?" And I said, "Well, he does concerts. . . ."

We recorded several albums with Cachao, beginning with *Master Sessions, Vol. 1*, which enjoyed critical success and won a Grammy (in fact, it won the year after Gloria won for *Mi Terra*). It was never about album sales with Crescent Moon and Cachao—he gave us instant credibility. Most important, the album brought a sound that was in danger of being lost to a new audience. Cachao was a link to the music I had grown up with in Cuba. I wanted so much to show this respect to my heritage and Latin culture and work with Cachao, someone I greatly admired as a musician and as a person. He also happened to be one of the nicest people I met in my whole life. We finally lost Cachao when he died at age eighty-nine in Coral Gables, Florida, in 2008.

Another of the nicest and most humble people I ever met was another Cuban legend, Celia Cruz, the Queen of Salsa. We'd worked with Celia in the Miami Sound Machine days. Years later she didn't have a record label and I wanted to sign her for Sony. I actually had the biggest fight I ever had with Sony over Celia. They didn't want me to sign her, saying she was too old. I did sign her, and she had a string of number one hits and won a fistful of Grammys before she died in 2003. It was a dream of mine to produce Celia Cruz. We made her first-ever music video and had a lot of fun.

Shakira and Ricky Martin are important, of course, in my career, but it was so important to me to help this Cuban legend. I am probably proudest of working with Celia and with Cachao, both artists whom the rest of the industry had written off as being too old. I don't think there's any such thing as being too old—someone's either a great artist or they aren't.

Helping Celia and Cachao also fit in with my feelings about venerating older members of society. They have a wealth of experience that we shouldn't ignore. They provide a link to the past that it's easy to lose. These are reasons I've always respected Japanese culture so much. Reading about Japan I'd always been drawn to aspects of the country that resonated with me. Respect for the family, especially elders, was one. I was very interested in the way they live, with large families often squeezed into small houses. When I'd been in the United States a few years I saved up money from performing and took an organized tour to Japan. I was fascinated to visit. It's fine to read about a place, but if you really want to know how somewhere ticks you've got to go see it.

It was interesting to see the way other people live. Foreign travel can be particularly inspiring to someone with an open mind and a willingness to learn. When Gloria and I got married I said we should go to Japan for our honeymoon, because we'd probably not have another chance, and we've probably been there ten times since.

Keep in mind when you're thinking about ideas that your greatest resource is you. You're an infinite source of talent and ideas. We continue to develop and even to renew and recycle our skill sets. It's a way of reinventing yourself and moving yourself forward. I'm a good example of that. I was always a musician, and I loved it. But early on, as the Miami Sound Machine began to gain a certain measure of success, I realized I could do more. And I wanted to do more, because I am a perfectionist and also because I am very energetic.

I would get frustrated sometimes with a show when the sound wasn't as good as it could have been or the lighting wasn't right. I started to get involved in more aspects of our work. It gave me a greater sense of security and also of satisfaction, because I was more in control of the quality of our work. Becoming a producer was a great way to recycle myself and my skill set, and to take myself to another level. I continued learning. If someone ever told me I couldn't be a producer, I either didn't hear it or I didn't listen. In the end I was doing everything. I was pretty confident that I could do what I put my mind to. I believed in myself and the idea of doing something different with my talents.

Why do we underestimate our own abilities to do more and to succeed at different tasks? It's easy to convince yourself that you have reached your level of competence, and that you had better stay there. We can all do so much more. First you have to believe in yourself and then you can be fertile ground which inspiration can grow.

CHAPTER TWENTY-SIX

Focus When Disaster Strikes

W hat happens when, as John Lennon put it, life happens to you while you're busy making other plans?

I loved touring with the Miami Sound Machine and Gloria. We saw the world, we met captains and kings and legions of loyal, loving fans, and we had an awful lot of fun along the way. And at the height of the band's success, we had a small child, our son, Nayib. As long as he was around Gloria and me, he wasn't the least bit bothered by being in different environments. Kids are like that. In fact, travel awakens a lot of talents and tastes in children as well as inspiring their parents. But there comes a point when children need a more stable environment, and by age six or seven, Nayib had reached that point.

That coincided with a time in my life when I felt like attempting something different. I was learning more and more about the music business and I certainly felt challenged to do something else, something different. I often felt frustrated that things were not as good as they could have been in our shows. I felt the need to step back and manage, an urge to produce and to perfect.

Gloria had fronted the Miami Sound Machine for a long time and was about to go out on her own, just as members of the band were ready to move on to other projects. And all that coincided with Nayib's needing to settle into school and a more constant routine. So I decided to become a stay-at-home dad.

I was starting to produce different artists and I found that I had a knack and a talent for it. I love all the aspects of producing. It is something that suits my temperament and my skill set very well: It demands a lot of attention to detail; it is creative; and you are responsible for the end result. I like to complete things.

When Gloria toured, we would fly to meet her on weekends for shows, or she'd fly home during breaks. It was rough, but it gave Nayib the stability and routine that he needed for a few years and it allowed me to develop my career as a producer. And I needed to support Gloria's dreams and her talents.

Anyone who knows anything about us knows that Gloria and I have never had any scandal attached to our names. There's an easy explanation for that: We've never done anything to cause a scandal. Really. You need to build your career on talent, not on gossip, if you want to be in it for the long haul. When we toured together our son was young, so as soon as the concert was over we would head back to the hotel and hit the sack. When Gloria toured without us, it was much the same. But Gloria didn't enjoy touring without us.

So eventually we went back on the road with her, and I again took over the day-to-day managing and producing of the show. I enjoyed this job too because I was able to use a lot of my different talents and skills, and I was still able to produce other artists.

All the sacrifices of touring were worth it. The best part of all was when Gloria would walk off the stage at the end of a show. Immediately after feeling the love and enthusiasm of her fans, still riding the incredible rush of adrenaline that performing gives, she would walk into our arms. Nayib and I would always be standing in the wings, waiting for her. In later years, our daughter, Emily, who was born in 1994, would join us as her mother walked off the stage.

In the winter of 1990, President George H. W. Bush invited us to the White House. We were thrilled, proud, and excited. Nayib, Gloria, and I had our picture taken with the President in the Oval Office, a photo that ran widely. As one newspaper caption so accurately put it, the world was in our hands, and we felt that way too! It was an incredible moment in our lives. It was the culmination of our dreams to be recognized by the president of our adopted country.

Little did we know that within twenty-four hours, our lives would be plunged into darkness.

Tommy Mottola invited us to New York City for a special dinner. I felt it was important to attend and convinced Gloria that we needed to go, so we drove to the city in our tour bus. The following day, we were headed to Syracuse. It was a gray, dull March day as we drove through Pennsylvania, and despite the lateness of the season, the roads were slick and snowy. Traffic was slow. Gloria was napping; Nayib was playing.

All of sudden, we heard a loud noise. I felt a shuddering, sickening jolt and the bus went completely dark. A tractor-trailer had plowed into our tour bus. Gloria called out for Nayib. I found him, shaken but fine. Gloria, however, couldn't move. When I reached her, she said she couldn't feel anything. I realized very quickly that we needed help, but the accident blocked traffic and it would be hours before Gloria could be evacuated. In the meantime, a woman came aboard the bus and held Gloria's neck in her hands and spoke softly to her. That woman probably saved Gloria from permanent paralysis.

No one else on the bus had been seriously injured, something I am grateful for to this day.

Gloria was finally taken by ambulance to a nearby hospital, where she was diagnosed with serious spinal fractures. Nayib, shaken and bruised, and with a broken collarbone, stuck close to my side. He and I went separately to the hospital in Scranton.

When we arrived at the hospital I was brought into a room where Gloria lay strapped to a board, her head and neck braced. She was completely immobile, paralyzed. The doctor said to me that Gloria had broken her back. As I looked at her, I felt my knees buckle and the room go black. The next thing I knew I was in a wheelchair myself. I was overcome with feelings of fear, helplessness—and guilt. Everything had happened so fast. Life can change in a split second.

I don't know how or where but I found the strength and the resources in myself to begin to turn the situation around. Once she was
stable, we had Gloria airlifted in an air ambulance to New York University in New York City. On what was the darkest day of our life as a family, as I held my son's hand and we flew through an overcast sky in
Pennsylvania, I caught a glimpse of the sun peeking through the clouds.
At that moment, I believed we were coming out of the dark, going into
the light. Although it was a desperate situation, there was hope. I reached
into my jacket pocket and on a slip of paper jotted down the phrase
"coming out of the dark." I stuck it into my jeans pocket, like a good-
luck charm, where it remained until I found it several months later. I had
to focus on the task at hand, the monumental task at hand: making sure
my wife would recover.

In New York, Gloria was operated on and two titanium rods were
fitted into her back to help fuse her broken vertebrae. For two long
weeks, she remained paralyzed. In what we consider a miracle, Gloria
began to regain feeling in her back and legs. As soon as that happened
we both knew that she would one day walk, run, dance, and even return
to performing. We were both very determined that this would happen.
But as she lay in that hospital bed we were a long way from that goal.
Julio Iglesias generously lent us his private plane, and we brought Gloria
back to Miami to begin the long process of recovery.

The accident put everything in our lives to the test. And as completely unprepared for it as we were, we were, in a strange way, ready for
it. We were as prepared as we could possibly be to face the challenge of
a long recovery.

When we built our house she put in an elevator because she said
someone in the family might need to use it one day. She had been thinking about her father and his long, debilitating illness. Our room is on the
second floor of the house. We used to race up the stairs to see who could
get there first. When we got home after the accident I was crying when
I put her in the elevator, but Gloria was a lot more prepared than me.
"Now you're going to win the race up the stairs," she said.

I've had some premonitions in my life. One time we were playing in

Los Angeles opening for Stevie Wonder. There were thousands of people there at a street festival, but at the third song, I had a weird feeling. Gloria was supposed to play about ten more songs, and I said, "Are you ready for a conga?" which was the way we closed the show, and she looked at me like, "What are you doing?" I said, "We need to get out of here." We played "Conga," and the minute we left the stage everything collapsed. The area where Gloria was performing was totally destroyed; people were injured.

After the bus accident we began by putting aside the thoughts of what we had so carefully planned. We had wanted another baby after the tour ended, but that idea would have to be put off for now, perhaps forever. We had other plans to branch out professionally, to start new businesses, but all that had to be put aside or on hold. We had to focus on the task at hand—Gloria's recovery. It was the only thing that mattered.

It's extraordinary how quickly your priorities can change in the face of a disaster like this. It also demonstrates just how important your good health is. As long as you enjoy good health, it's easy to take it for granted. When it's lost, even temporarily, you'd give anything to have it back.

I spent six months helping Gloria with very basic tasks. The first time she brushed her teeth for herself she was crying. How often in those long months did we hear the phrase, "No, it can't be done"? "No, Gloria will never walk again." "No, Gloria will never dance again." "No, Gloria will never be the same again." We'd heard "no" before. We had never taken "no" for any answer earlier. Why start now? Don't tell us we can't.

Gloria's recovery was a team effort. We focused so hard on her getting well. She spent long hours in therapy and in the gym. She rarely left home. Her spirits remained good, admirably so, but it became increasingly difficult for her to keep a positive outlook, because progress in this type of recovery is so slow. Agonizingly slow. It is literally one step at a time, one foot in front of the other.

About four months after the accident, I suggested we go to the studio. Neither one of us had really left home for a long time. Gloria was uncharacteristically glum. She needed to focus on something else besides her back, I realized. As were driving to the studio, I reached into my jeans pocket to get money to pay a toll and there was the slip of paper I had put there four months ago during the helicopter flight to New York. (I'm amazed that paper survived so many washes!) I showed Gloria the paper. The song "Coming out of the Dark" practically wrote itself, and it was a giant step forward in Gloria's recovery.

We always found solace in our music, and that day in the studio, seeing Gloria, I felt completely confident that she would return to the stage, although that was still months away. As much as we counted our blessings and were grateful that Gloria was not paralyzed, that she could walk and was becoming more independent again, we would not be satisfied until Gloria could return to her former self. This is where we saw more than ever the power of positive thinking and of believing in yourself.

Gloria's accident was in March of 1990. In January of 1991 she sang "Coming out of the Dark" at the American Music Awards. It was an incredibly moving experience, and Gloria felt the love of the audience, who stood and applauded as she came onto the stage. That song became a number one single for Gloria. It was the public celebration of her survival and her return.

Looking back I can say that the accident and recovery gave us so much, although at the time we went through some extremely dark days. All the life lessons I learned from it I have applied to my professional life. The main lesson is that I can't be deterred by "no"; I have to take matters into my own hands, and I always have to believe in and to visualize a successful outcome. So many times we heard a negative prognosis for Gloria: all the things that professionals were predicting she wouldn't be able to do as a result of her accident. I guess everyone was preparing us for the worst. We faced the worst, took it on, and beat it.

It reinforced my feeling about living in the moment. Never miss a chance to hug someone, to kiss someone. To tell those you love that you love them. For in one moment were on top of the world. We'd just visited the White House. Our careers were going great. The next, everything we worked for meant nothing while there was a chance my wife might never walk again. But she came through the ordeal stronger than ever.

CHAPTER TWENTY-SEVEN

Manage Success by Not Standing Still

All my life I've run around keeping numerous balls in the air at any one time. When I first moved to this country I juggled my job at Bacardi with high school and playing the accordion in my little band. Over the years the stakes may have changed but the principles remained the same. I went from working for tips in a restaurant to playing with and managing an internationally successful band. I went from the mailroom at Bacardi to a six-figure salary in their Latin marketing department. All the time I was moving forward. In juggling, when you stop the motion, the balls fall to earth with a thud. When everything in my professional life started to snowball and other business opportunities presented themselves, something had to give. And it was my day job.

Bacardi was so rich in opportunity for me, and I felt valued, and also felt that anything I wanted to try my hand at in the company, I could. I was promoted quickly and often. I liked Bacardi's corporate culture. Bacardi was very flexible with its employees, in part because the people running the company know how important it is to develop good professionals. Had I been working somewhere else, I might not have had the time or had supervisors who allowed me to get my work done for them but also work on my own projects—namely music—at the same time.

There were more and more opportunities to make music. I had worked at Bacardi for more than ten years, the only time in my life when

I really worked as an employee. In 1980, when the time was ripe to leave and to dedicate myself fully to music—and also when I felt fully ready to take the leap—I told my bosses what I planned to do. "My love is music. I want to go out on my own now." I asked one thing in return. "If things don't work out, can I come back?" And they told me, "As many times as you like. Whatever you want to do." Don't burn your bridges!

I appreciated that amazing show of support from my company. It was also a validation that I'd done my job well and that they valued me, not just my work. As it turned out, of course, I didn't ever return to Bacardi as an employee, but we have maintained a long and fruitful relationship. Bacardi often sponsors our tours and events. The work contacts you make early in your career can be invaluable later in life. You simply never know whom you're going to run into in the future, so don't go burning any bridges! As I've said, we sell a lot of Bacardi rum in our restaurants, so the relationship is still working for all concerned.

I was never content with having just one thing on the go at a time. Gloria and I looked for opportunities to secure our future as a family. We were always careful with money, and since the fate of musicians depends on the taste of audiences, we knew we had to save our money. As hard as we worked, we could never be sure we'd be around forever.

Gloria and I always saved, but when our music really started to take off, we realized that there was a lot more we could do with the money we were earning than just leave it in the bank. We were interested in real estate, and not just because conventional wisdom says it's a good way to make your money work for you. We knew that in most economic climates real estate is a sound investment—although a long-term one—and that there was plenty of opportunity in Miami. Our first purchase was a duplex in northwest Miami (which we still own—we're kind of sentimental like that).

We loved Miami Beach long before most of the rest of the world discovered it through *Miami Vice* and the glossy fashion magazines. When we had a chance to buy on Ocean Drive, a lot of the area was run-down and neglected—but oh, my God, there were some beautiful buildings there, just begging to be recovered and renovated and taken care of.

In 1985, we bought a low-rise built in the 1930s, right in the heart of the historic Art Deco district. That was the start of our real estate business. And it was also our first foray outside of the music business. We've continued to invest in real estate over the years, and those investments led us into other concerns, like the restaurant and hotel businesses. We started investing in residential properties and then branched out into commercial properties. We kept a very close eye on our real estate investments, and we bought properties in areas we knew and where we believed there was growth potential.

Even though it wasn't our initial intention to get into real estate big-time, our investments mushroomed. Miami is our hometown, and we began to invest during a downturn in the industry. That's one smart way to do things—buy cheap—but you also have to have faith in your investments. Real estate can be a risky business, but there are many ways to mitigate the risks. Chief among them is knowing where you're putting your money. You're not going to invest in something just so that the value of it remains the same. You may as well keep your money under your mattress. But you're also not going to invest in a place sight unseen—at least, I hope you're not! So do your homework.

One of our biggest real estate purchases was out of necessity. In the late 1980s, we realized it made sense to have our own production facility, so we bought a building on Bird Road, a spacious and well-maintained property that had previously housed doctors' offices. There we built our recording studio, Crescent Moon. It was part of a bigger plan: creating Miami's Motown. I wanted the studio not just for Gloria and the Miami Sound Machine, but to record other artists as well. That's an example of need coupled with a vision. We needed our own place, but I also knew that I could build a bigger business on top of that business. Every business can be a step to another. That building now holds our recording studios, video production and editing facilities, studios, and office space.

We didn't go out and buy a recording studio as soon as we could. We made thoughtful investments, sometimes based solely on opportunity, and other times motivated in part by need, as with the studio. As Estefan Enterprises grew and diversified, we needed to consolidate our corporate offices, so we bought a building on Miami Beach, and when we outgrew that we bought an entire four-story office building in South Beach. Out of that building we run all of Estefan Enterprises. It's centrally located (and not far from where we live, either). It originally housed Arquitectonica, the internationally renowned architecture firm responsible for so many of the new buildings in south Florida, like the American Airlines Arena, and great buildings around the world, like the dramatic Westin hotel in Times Square New York. Ours is a beautiful building and was in very good shape when we bought it.

I wouldn't say that I'm an expert on real estate, but I do know a couple of rules of thumb that have helped me in the real estate business. First, making a good purchase (at a good price) isn't enough. You have to invest in the upkeep of the property or it will lose its value. Second, don't fall in love with a building that you have bought as an investment. If you do, you won't be able to sell it when you need to make a profit. Another key thing is that you don't have to be an expert on the whole business, but you should be an expert on your own investments.

Although I am encouraging you to grow, you need to do so at the right pace, one step at a time. If you are in it for the long haul and not just the quick flip, you have to be patient. Our first offices were in the garage at my parents' house, then in a small building.

As we were getting involved in these other businesses, our lives, both personal and professional, were moving along at a fast clip. Gloria had already been a solo artist for quite a while, our son was growing, and I was producing and managing more and more artists.

We had created Estefan Enterprises always with a view to branching out. We established the company in May 1986, even before we got into our other ventures. We knew we had to keep our business affairs in order, and formally setting up a company was a good way to start. Estefan Enterprises has businesses in music and entertainment, real estate, and hospitality. But as you can see, it didn't happen overnight.

Our real estate investments have grown so much over the past twenty years that we now have an entire division of Estefan Enterprises that handles real estate. (Yet we're not a real estate company.) Real estate was something both Gloria and I have a feel for, and we've enjoyed all aspects of the business—and it is a complicated business involving financing, contracts, and city codes. It also involves dealing with people in different professions, so to be successful at it you need to be fairly versatile and open.

ANOTHER BUSINESS VENTURE NOT RELATED to our core business of music and entertainment is the Larios on the Beach restaurant. I credit Gloria with the idea of getting into this particular venture. She said to me that Miami had been very good to us and we should give something back and make a serious investment in something we loved in the city we loved. And since I am so strongly motivated to share and promote our culture, this seemed like a great idea.

The Larios family owned Casa Larios, a very successful Cuban restaurant in Miami and one of our favorite places to eat. For Gloria and me, Cuban cuisine is the ultimate comfort food. When friends would visit from all over the world, they'd want to go to South Beach, which in the 1980s and 1990s was being discovered, or rediscovered, by tourists, and a lot of our friends would ask us to take them out for Cuban food. Since South Beach is a mecca for the young and beautiful—and health conscious—we were told over and over that Cuban food wouldn't appeal to the people who liked to hang out in South Beach, in particular on Ocean Drive. Cuban food can be pretty heavy, that's true, but there is really a surprising variety of things to choose from more on the healthy side. Not everything is fried—there are plenty of vegetables, rice and beans, plantains, grilled fish. We love it, we were convinced it would be a hit, and, once again, we weren't going to take no for an answer.

There were a couple of buildings on Ocean Drive that we wanted to buy and restore to their Art Deco glory, so we convinced the Larios family to join forces with us, and Larios on the Beach was born. By the third day after the opening, there were lines around the block of people wanting to get in. Maybe it was the food, maybe it was the novelty, or—I won't deny it—maybe there was the curiosity factor: What was Gloria Estefan's restaurant going to be like? In any case, it was an instant hit.

What makes something a lasting success has a lot more to do with your vision than with any trend or gimmick. We were promoting something we love—our culture—and we believed in it wholeheartedly. In the case of real estate, a good investment requires overseeing and upkeep, continuous renovation. In the case of hospitality—restaurants and hotels—it's pretty similar: You need to pay attention to your investment and keep upgrading and updating.

When you are working in the restaurant world you're faced with a popularity contest every day. Consumers in a major city like Miami have thousands of places to choose from. If one day they decide to try your place, you have to put yourself in the best position to have them return. Take care of your customers; keep surprising them and they'll come back for more. That means the food has to be great—every day. That means the service has to be great—every day. It means your menu has to remain fresh and relevant. It's all hard work and attention to detail.

WE BOUGHT THE CARDOZO HOTEL around the same time we opened Larios on the Beach. It's also on Ocean Drive and has been around since the Art Deco era of the 1930s. What a beautiful building! When Gloria and I were first dating, we didn't have much money. We used to like to go over to Miami Beach to walk around, and we always admired the architecture. I used to tell Gloria that one day I would buy her the Cardozo. We didn't miss the chance when it came, but that investment was more than just delivering on a romantic promise. We saw plenty of opportunity there, right on Ocean Drive. The Cardozo is now a boutique hotel with its own restaurant, the Cardozo Bar and Grill.

The hospitality business presents so many opportunities. It's a really challenging but also a really creative business. For me, it combines so many of the skills I've built up over the years, and I find it so fulfilling. We've even been able to branch out and franchise one of our restaurants.

Some executives from Disney invited Gloria and me to dinner one evening in the mid-1990s to discuss the possibility of our opening a restaurant in Downtown Disney. I had been thinking around that time what hunger people have for the past, how nostalgic people can be, so their timing was good! This would be different from Larios on the Beach because in a way it would be a tribute to our parents and to the Cuba they had told us about and asked us to never forget. And what a great opportunity for us to share our culture with a much wider audience.

That's how Bongos Cuban Café came to be. It was one of those ideas that comes about and happens when you least expect it to. Bongos Cuban Café has Cuban cuisine, Cuban design—walls lined with tropical art, vintage photos, and yes, bongos—and plays Cuban music. As soon as it opened in Disney, it was an instant hit, as Larios on the Beach had been. By the end of the first year, more than seven hundred thousand customers had been to Bongos Cuban Café in Disney World. It's been a great partnership—we share revenues with Disney but even more important, we own the Bongos Cuban Café brand. And most important of all, we represent our culture and honor our heritage in a way that would make our parents proud. The younger generations of Cuban-Americans, like my kids, didn't know as much about their culture as we would have liked, so this was also a great way to foster pride in the culture among young Cubans.

Less than five years after the first Bongos Cuban Café opened, when the American Airlines Arena in downtown Miami was built, we opened a second Bongos Cuban Café adjoining the arena. (You can't miss it—the giant pineapple roof greets all the cruise ships as they come into the Port of Miami!) Bongos Cuban Café, both in Miami and at Disney, are highly successful clubs, hosting large-scale events, often headlined by top entertainers. And not too long ago, we exported Bonguitos—you can now get Cuban coffee and other delicacies in Puerto Vallarta.

I believe that a successful business is one that never stands still. That doesn't mean that a business has to eat up the competition. Not standing still means that the greatest enemy of successful business is complacency. That means working hard to improve what you already have, to make sure you have the best possible restaurant or bookstore or car-cleaning business possible. And we never expanded or brought in new ventures for the sake of it—everything made sense within the parameters of what we were trying to do. The businesses fit within my basic skill set, and I was able to expand my knowledge by remaining willing to learn. Through it all I understand that the key to every business is the people involved.

CHAPTER TWENTY-EIGHT

Be the Boss

I t's a truism that businesses are about people—the employees and the customers. But you'd be surprised how many businesses seem to forget it. You might not be surprised if you've recently been the victim of some ridiculous customer service mishap, if someone's been rude to you on an airplane or at a restaurant, or if your employer has treated you like a piece of furniture. It happens all the time. But I can honestly say that I've always been committed to growing our businesses because of our employees. We could never have achieved what we have without them. They have devoted their time and energy to us for many years, and ensuring that they have a livelihood is vitally important to me. I feel a sense of responsibility for them.

And I do for our customers. Businesses need to be ready to change with the times and also to grow with their customers. Whatever your product or business, at some point your customers are going to want something new and improved or simply something different. The trick is realizing that long enough before they do to have time to do something about it.

Let's look at employees first. The boss-employee relationship is a two-way street. Being a boss means you're at the service of others. You have to be aware of employees' needs (salary, holidays, benefits) as well as their aspirations (new challenges, promotions). Being a boss is synonymous with being a leader. You need to excite your employees about work and to "infect" them with your enthusiasm for what you are all doing together. A true leader knows how to inspire and get the best out of people by giving the best of him- or herself. Again (how many times have we come back to this?), positive thinking is key. That attitude has helped me get the best out of myself and out of all the people I work with. It's contagious. People are inspired—and they feel more confident—if they see that the guy at the top has faith in what you're all doing.

The best leadership is by example, so be prepared to do the heavy lifting. As I've written, I've tended bar, set up mics, cables, the sound board, helped load equipment onto trucks, and anything else that has needed to be done. I'm a very hands-on boss, I think everyone who works for me would agree with that. I'm also something of a perfectionist. While you're demanding your best of yourself and those around you, at the same time you can create a positive atmosphere of encouragement and good energy. It must be horrible to work at something that you don't feel passionate about, or to have a boss who doesn't encourage you or appreciate you.

There are few things more demoralizing than doing something you hate or working for someone who doesn't encourage you. People who love what they do don't worry about the little extras, and they don't spend the whole day watching the clock, yearning for five p.m. They gladly do what needs to be done, and they work as many hours as necessary to get the job done.

It's also important, especially in tough economic times like these, to be frugal with your resources and keep costs low. If you spend excessively, especially when employees' needs aren't met, you will put your business at risk and shake the confidence of those who work for you. In our case, even when the music business suffered losses, we didn't fire people. We were able to move them into other jobs. Not all businesses can do that, of course, but it is important to be conscious that you need to take care of your employees and their employment as much as possible.

Most of all, treat employees and colleagues well. Treating people well will also earn you a reputation as a good person and boss—and never underestimate the value of a good reputation.

You also can't be shy about managing people. You're the boss, after all, and that means you have to tell people when they are doing a good job, just as you have to let them know when their work is not good enough. A good boss has to be demanding. Don't be afraid of pushing employees to do and be their best.

I recall a meeting we had recently at one of our restaurants. Sales were down, even though we were getting roughly the same flow of customers. I spent some time watching the staff and I thought they really weren't providing very good service to our customers. We held a meeting and I shared my observations with them. First and foremost, I reminded them of the important role they play. Waiters are there to serve and to help customers relax and enjoy themselves. They are also the business's sales force. They weren't filling customers' water glasses or suggesting different dishes or specials very enthusiastically. I suggested they offer something that the customer might not have tried. "Would you like a mojito? If you don't like it, it's on me."

"Why don't you offer another drink or a dessert?" I said. "Don't wait for the customer to ask." I also pointed out the fact that the higher the bill, the better the tip. And the better the service, the more likely the customer is to come back. Constructive criticism is important, but there is never a need or an excuse to tear an employee down.

Effective hiring is a vital part of being the boss. When you have a position you need to fill, sometimes the right candidate is right before your eyes. Finding a great employee can sometimes mean developing the ones you already have. It may be that there's a potential recruit for that position in a relatively junior position who could grow into the job. I believe we underestimate our own abilities to do more and to succeed at different tasks.

On the employee's side, it's easy to convince yourself that you're at your level of competence, and that you had better stay there. I think we can all do so much more. When we are looking to grow a business, almost the first thing we think we need to increase is personnel. That isn't necessarily so. I don't think people should be overworked, but many times we do not give our staff or employees the challenges they would relish. Yes, that's right. People like to be given *more* work, especially if it includes added responsibility and the increased authority to meet those responsibilities. Why hire more people when you can work with the same group, especially if it is a loyal and cohesive group?

The arguments for not staffing up are very important, especially in periods of growth. You have to be really careful about not overstaffing. It's better to be understaffed with eager, qualified people and keep them motivated. You can increase staff at any time, but having to downscale and lay people off sends a message that you haven't planned very carefully. And it can be very demoralizing to those who stay.

Using the staff you have and seeing how you can help them grow their talents by retraining or recycling their skill sets is a big but also an important challenge. You need to be resourceful to figure out where people fit, and it is a great opportunity for you to allow your employees to figure out for themselves where they fit and what more they can do for your organization. You may have to pay those people more than they would make elsewhere, but it will be worth it. And it is still usually cheaper for you to pay a few employees well rather than to take on an army and have to pay salaries and benefits to underworked people just to keep them employed while you try to grow the business.

That said, never try to keep salaries too low. It's really important to pay people what they deserve. And I don't think people feel overworked when they are highly motivated and challenged. But keep in mind that money motivates only to an extent. It buys services from employees but it won't buy their long-term loyalty. Understanding employees and their needs and aspirations will do that.

Some of the best ideas I've had have to do with my staff and people I've hired over the years. It's hard to find good people. It's a bit like getting married, actually. There may be an immediate attraction or appeal, but it really does take time and effort to get to know people. Once you do, you certainly want to hang on to them.

I have been very fortunate in my choice of employees. I think that is because I am always looking for highly motivated people. Frank Amadeo is now my right-hand man and president of Estefan Enterprises. I'd known Frank for years before I hired him in 1992, when he left a radio station in south Florida. As far as hiring Frank was concerned, the thing that struck me was the fact that he couldn't speak Spanish. The very foundations of our company are firmly entrenched in the Hispanic community, and we do a lot of our business in Spanish. But obviously I liked the guy (he's the president of my company!), so I gave him a chance working in media relations under Gloria's sister. I think a lot of bosses would have looked no farther than Frank's then-lack of Spanish and not hired him. (Frank is the perfect example of the reverse crossover!) I trust Frank with my life and, even more important, with my family. I know that if anything would happen to me, Frank would be there for them. Right after 9/11, when everyone was skittish about the state of things, Frank came to me and offered to take a cut in salary. I did not accept his offer, of course, but I was deeply touched by his loyalty and commitment.

A lot of the key positions in my company are held by women (many of whom are also immigrants). We shouldn't have one-dimensional views of people and where their talents lie or what their work habits might be because of their sex or background. And this is extremely important—and one of the great things about this country—there are laws that prohibit discrimination in hiring, housing, and other areas on the basis of race, gender, sexual orientation, religious beliefs, etc. . . . . You shouldn't discriminate not only because you might miss out on potentially great employees—but because discrimination is against the law!

You'll find highly motivated people come in all shapes and sizes, colors, and so on. Only a few times have I hired people and they didn't work out. You can make some unconventional hires at times, but people need to be qualified. I meet people and I file them away. I'm my own headhunting service. You can't hire people and keep them in reserve, but you have to be thinking about growth and eventually getting more staff. When the timing isn't right, you simply have to wait, and keep in touch with or keep track of potential future hires.

When looking for employees, be counterintuitive and trust your instincts. Look for ambition and look for motivation. Few people are more motivated than parents and people with family responsibilities. Mothers and single mothers especially can have a hard time combining career and child raising. It's especially tough for single moms and I have enormous respect for them. There is no easy way to work and raise children all by yourself, but I encourage employers not to look at single mothers as a liability. On the contrary, you'll find that single mothers—and women in general—are more organized than most men. They have to be.

Single mothers often make excellent employees. They have the best motivation. I've always tried to be flexible with people's particular situations. To the extent that you can, without invading people's privacy, you as an employer should be aware of your employees' needs. There have been times when our offices look like a nursery because employees have had to bring in their children because the kids are sick or their caregivers didn't show up or for any number of reasons. I don't mind having a crib in the office or having an employee come in later or leave earlier for personal reasons. Employees remember your kindness and understanding. And they especially remember that you have taken their lives beyond work into consideration.

Don't close the door on potential employees because they seem to have a tougher personal situation than others. Giving someone a chance may result in a big payoff for you and the employee. Sometimes you try to move people out of their areas of expertise and the results are spectacular—or disastrous. But it is something often worth trying. You just have to keep an eye on how people are doing. You have to manage them, and that takes time and commitment.

I once put an ad in the newspaper for a chef. A woman showed up. She said she couldn't cook, but she had six kids and she needed a job badly. She said, "You hire me and I'm going to be the best chef you've ever had." Well, this may contradict what I just said about hiring qualified people, but I also said you should use your instincts, and in this case instinct trumped the qualifications. I took a risk and hired the woman, and she learned quickly on the job and became a great cook. She knew

I was taking a chance in hiring her, and my trust was a great motivating force. Not as great as having to feed six kids, but substantial nonetheless.

There is nothing I prize more highly in another person than loyalty. There's a reason I have had the same doctor and the same dentist—not to mention Gloria, the same wife—for over thirty years. They know me well; I know them well. They treat me well; I treat them well. Loyalty.

Loyalty isn't just about staying in a relationship a long time, though. Like everything else, it takes work. It's about knowing and growing with others. It is about being supportive of them, and about them being supportive of you. It is also being forgiving when need be. Loyalty is a two-way street. And it means sharing in successes and being supportive in times of failure. You can't do anything great alone. There are plenty of people who have helped you and who will help you along the way. Don't ever forget them. Success is most enjoyable when it is shared. And a burden is borne more easily when it is shouldered by you and others.

Starting with Bacardi and moving on to Estefan Enterprises, all my professional success has always been as part of a larger team, both as an employee and an employer. Throughout there's been a constant: As I've added responsibilities in managing other people I've had to get better at managing myself.

At the recording of *El Último Adiós,* a tribute and homage to the victims and families of September 11 / En la grabación de *El último adiós*, un tributo y homenaje a las víctimas y a las familias de septiembre 11

MAGGIE RODRIGUEZ

Emilio and Shakira recording in the studio / Shakira y Emilio grabando en el estudio

MAGGIE RODRIGUEZ

Ricky Martin and Emilio at the taping of *El Último Adiós* / Ricky Martín y Emilio en la grabación de *El último adiós*

Emilio and Jennifer Lopez /
Emilio y Jennifer Lopez

Emilio, Gloria, Ricky
Martin, Jennifer Lopez,
Tommy Mottola at the
Sony GRAMMY Party /
Emilio, Gloria, Ricky
Martin, Jennifer Lopez,
Tommy Mottola en la
fiesta de Sony de los
GRAMMYs

Gloria, Celia Cruz, and Emilio in the
recording studio / Gloria, Celia Cruz,
y Emilio en el estudio de grabación

Julio Iglesias, Gloria, and Emilio /
Julio Iglesias, Gloria, y Emilio

Emilio and Andy Garcia playing
bongos at Lario's on the Beach /
Emilio y Andy Garcia tocando
bongos en Lario's en la playa

Israel "Cachao" Lopez and
Emilio / Israel "Cachao"
Lopez y Emilio

Emilio, Gloria, and
"Cachao" / Emilio,
Gloria, y "Cachao"

Emilio and Thalia /
Emilio y Thalia

Emilio, Marcos Avila, Cristina Saralegui

Lili Estefan and Emilio / Lili Estefan y Emilio

Gloria, Emilio, and Pope John Paul II at the Vatican in Rome / Gloria, Emilio, y el Papa Juan Pablo II en El Vaticano en Roma

Emilio, Nelson Mandela, Gloria, and Nayib in South Africa / Emilio, Nelson Mandela, Gloria, y Nayib en Sudáfrica

Emilio, Gloria, and Quincy Jones / Emilio, Gloria, y Quincy Jones

Emilio and Sylvester Stallone on the movie set of *The Specialist* / Emilio y Sylvester Stallone en la filmación de la película *The Specialist*

Madonna, David Geffen, Emilio, and Gloria, New Year's Eve at Gianni Versace's mansion on Miami Beach / Madonna, David Geffen, Emilio, y Gloria, Año Nuevo en la mansión de Gianni Versace en Miami Beach

Pitbull, Emilio, and Sean "Puffy" Combs at the Latin Billboard Awards /Pitbull, Emilio, y Sean "Puffy" Combs en los Latin Billboard Awards

Emilio and Donald Trump / Emilio y Donald Trump

Emilio and Muhammad Ali / Emilio y Muhammad Ali

EMILIO ESTEFAN

Emilio, President George H. W. Bush, and Gloria / Emilio, el Presidente George H. W. Bush, y Gloria

EMILIO ESTEFAN

Gloria, Emily, President Bill Clinton, First Lady Hillary Rodham Clinton, and Emilio during Christmas in Washington / Gloria, Emily, el Presidente Bill Clinton, Primera Dama Hillary Rodham Clinton, y Emilio en Navidad en Washington

EMILIO ESTEFAN

President Bill Clinton, First Lady Hillary Rodham Clinton, Gloria, Emilio, Chelsea Clinton, and Nayib at the Clinton Inaugural / Presidente Bill Clinton, Primera Dama Hillary Rodham Clinton, Gloria, Emilio, Chelsea Clinton, y Nayib en la Inauguración de los Clinton

Emilio and President George W. Bush aboard *Air Force I* / Emilio y el Presidente George W. Bush en *Air Force I*

EMILIO ESTEFAN

EMILIO ESTEFAN

President Barack Obama, Emilio, and First Lady Michelle Obama / Presidente Barack Obama, Emilio, y Primera Dama Michelle Obama

Queen Sophia, King Juan Carlos of Spain, and Emilio / Reina Sofía, Rey Juan Carlos de España, y Emilio

Emilio Estefan receives Honorary Doctorate of Music degree from University of Miami, with UM trustee Gloria Estefan / Emilio Estefan recibe un doctorado honorario en musica de la Universidad de Miami con Gloria Estefan, Fideicomisaria de la Universidad

Emilio with his Ellis Island Medal of Honor / Emilio con su medalla del honor de Isla de Ellis

Emilio receiving his star on the Hollywood Walk of Fame / Emilio recibiendo su estrella en el Paseo de la Fama en Hollywood

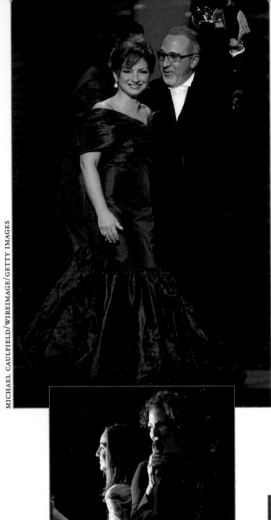

Emilio receives his 19th GRAMMY at the 2008 Latin GRAMMY Awards / Emilio recibiendo su 19th GRAMMY en los 2008 Premios GRAMMY Latinos

Emilio and Nayib give Gloria a big kiss after she receives a lifetime achievement recognition at the Alma Awards / Emilio y Nayib dan un gran beso a Gloria después de recibir en los Alma Awards, un premio honorífico a toda su carrera

Emilio's favorite members of Miami Sound Machine: Emily and Gloria / Para Emilio, las dos integrantes favoritas del Miami Sound Machine: Emily y Gloria

Gloria's triumphant return to the stage after her paralyzing bus accident / El retorno triunfante de Gloria al escenario después de si aterrador accidente de bus

CHAPTER TWENTY-NINE

Manage Yourself

F irst I want to address a misconception people have about being
the boss. They'll say they want to be in charge, have their own
company, and be the boss. They'll say they don't want to have to answer
to anyone. If that's your motivation, I'd advise you to find a good company and remain an employee. Because you're wrong. If you're the boss,
and especially if you're the owner of a company, you're accountable to
everyone. *Everyone.* You want to be left alone, you'd be better off staying
an employee, answerable only to your immediate superior. A boss is an
example, a role model, and often a mentor.

When you're the ultimate boss, you're the boss twenty-four hours a
day, and at the same time you're the company's number one employee.
You can't take a day off from being the last word in the company—no
one delegates every decision. Sure, you're your own boss (every employee
has a boss, right?), but you're everyone else's boss too, and that's hard
work. In order to do the best job managing your team, however large it
is, you need to make sure you do a great job managing your most important employee, yourself. (That applies if you're a freelancer working on
your own too!)

There are few things tougher than being a boss. It's really a vocation—
it's a special set of skills and you have to have the knack to do it. Where
do you acquire those skills? Sure, you can go to a fancy college and get

an MBA, but there's no such thing as "boss school." It's all about experience and judgment, attributes you gather over the course of a career. And you need a lot of self-discipline and, back to that word again, *vision*. You need to constantly articulate your vision and be able to communicate it to your employees. You need to make them a part of the dream.

A good entrepreneur naturally feels a sense of ownership of the idea and the company as a whole, an ability and a willingness to change and improve the company. As the boss, you need to communicate that you feel this way. And you have to get employees to share in this vision and have a sense of ownership for it. Share the big-picture vision of growth with your employees. That way they feel that their future, their security, depends in large part on their own efforts, which, of course, it does.

If you do want to be a boss and don't mind shouldering the responsibility that comes with it, there's nothing like working for yourself rather than as a cog in a corporate wheel. I've worked for corporations like Sony and Bacardi and also for myself, and people ask me what's the difference. It's a big difference. And if you can, I think you should always work for yourself.

Some people like the stability of a nine-to-five job that they don't have to take home with them. I respect that, but that's not me. It's much better that you work for yourself. You can give your creativity free rein. You can go with your instinct when your instinct is telling you to sign this artist or buy that hotel or open this restaurant. You don't need to get approval from any committee. This is not to say, of course, that you should act recklessly, but I need to have the freedom to succeed or fail on my own terms.

One lesson I learned in moving from a corporation to working for myself was to keep connections in my life. Well, it also works the other way. If someone has worked for me and then gone out to work for themselves, I like to offer my assistance. I can name hundreds of people I've maintained my connections with. If people stay with us they can move a long way in the company. A Miami Sound Machine road manager went on to manage Bongos Cuban Café; Gloria's road manager became the general manager at the Cardozo Hotel.

*   *   *

SO YOU'RE THE BOSS. YOU manage your employees well, you're loyal, you hire creatively but sensibly. Usually. And presumably you're good at the creative stuff and the Xs and Os of your business. Or you've hired good people who can do that for you. Finally there's this other key component to being a good boss, and that's managing yourself. Being your own boss, in other words. Actually it shouldn't be the last thing you think about but the first.

It starts with another one of those attributes that are taken for granted, and one of the most important skills for a boss: Be a good listener. A lot of people, once they have reached the peak of their profession or their company, get carried away with the wonderfulness of themselves and start to ignore what got them to that position. You can be sure they didn't do it all by themselves. They had a lot of help from their colleagues. So keep listening to what they have to say. And let people talk. It's amazing what you will learn. And more important still, listening is also a sign of respect.

Be open to people and their ideas. You need to be confident enough in yourself and your ideas that you can listen to what other people think. You can learn from everyone you work with. It's as valuable to talk to your interns about what they know and are learning in school as it is to talk to people who have been in the business for decades. And make sure they know you're listening. This isn't window dressing. Listening to what people say is a vital element in being a successful boss. Listening is underrated!

Lots of successful businessmen say you should take a successful model and copy it. It's not a bad idea when it comes to people either. Look to successful people whom you admire and follow their lead. There is nothing like having a mentor. I have had a few over the years and two really stand out for me. My admiration for Quincy Jones knows no limits. Quincy has had an extraordinary career, working with some of the greatest names in music in the last half century. We met when he did a Spanish version of "We Are the World" and asked Gloria and me to be on it. Of all Quincy's talents, most of all he is an extraordinary human being. He is a great example to me and to so many others.

Quincy is Emily's godfather. When Emily was born he was working on a television special and he wanted Gloria to be featured in it, but she'd had the baby only two days before. Quincy said Gloria could appear from our house. He took one look at little Emily and he said, "With all respect to you, I'm going to be the godfather of this baby." Quincy loves life and loves his friends. We talk a lot about life and history. We have a lot in common because of our minority status. Quincy had to go to Paris to kick-start his career, and we had a similar experience in Europe.

Quincy called me the other day. He was getting on a plane to go to Switzerland and he said, "I'm just calling you to tell you how much I love you." He has his priorities right—it's about humanity for him; fame he doesn't take seriously.

The other giant figure to me has been Phil Ramone. He's such a creative guy in a range of musical styles. The way he produced, the way he changed sounds . . . I learned so much from him. Phil's actually the only guy to produce Gloria other than me, so he must be special, right? He is quiet, unpretentious, a class act.

As an employee and as a boss you have to constantly be learning from people, improving yourself. You need to set goals not just for your business but also for your own professional development. You are the expert on your own idea, but that alone won't make you an expert on every aspect of your chosen field. Knowledge is an important tool. If you are going into a new field, learn as much as you can about it, and if you are expanding your business, make sure that you keep abreast of what is going on and that you are up-to-date. There are plenty of ways to inform yourself—books, seminars, courses. And, of course, research on the Internet is one of the most valuable tools we have nowadays, although you've got to use your judgment—there's a lot of cyber junk out there too. Use your street savvy—and if you don't have any, be sure to develop some.

You should never miss an opportunity to learn something else. You don't have to become an expert on every single aspect of business, but don't miss an opportunity to get someone to explain what he does, be it the company accountant, a production assistant, whoever. Always take the opportunity to learn. And not just within your own company. There is so much you can learn from any business, even something that appears to have nothing in common with what you do. If you are already well versed in one area of a business, there is nothing stopping you from learning more and getting a more comprehensive understanding of the entire business.

Just as it's important to keep moving and be busy, to diversify and to be willing to take on new projects, it's also important to know your limitations. I take on only about 10 percent of what I am offered. For me, it's a lot more important to have that 10 percent be successful than to have 100 percent failure. Take the word "mediocre" out of your vocabulary. Learn to say no. It can really take the wind out of your sails if you overcommit and underdeliver.

In today's extremely complex business environment, good legal and financial advice is critically important. It's often amazingly expensive but it will be money well spent. A referral is a very good way to find good lawyers, tax experts, and banks and other financial institutions willing to do business with you. Of course, getting professional advice shouldn't stop you from educating yourself on taxes, investments, and contracts. You should definitely learn as much as you can about all of that. Otherwise, how will you know when you are getting good advice?

No matter how good the advice you get, however, the decisions you make will be your own, and they will determine success or failure. When you have employees, that puts a lot of pressure on you, because people are relying on you not to screw it up. When your employees are also your family members, the stakes are higher still.

CHAPTER THIRTY

Work with Family

Marriage and children are fantastic goals, of course. The more people who are part of your life, the more comforting and exciting it should be. But it's more complicated too. Where does your personal life fit into your professional life and vice versa? When you are an entrepreneur, the line is often blurred between the personal and the professional. Often there's no line at all and your time is never truly your own.

Family and the people in your life will be integral to your success or failure, whether or not they're directly involved in your business. Their lives, their joys, sorrows, problems, and dreams—they will all affect your life. You need to get the members of your family on your side before you can consider getting anyone else involved. Your business is likely to absorb most of your time, so unless everyone is on the same page there will be tensions. And you always have to put their interests and well-being first. Most likely, your family, like mine, has always been your motivation and inspiration.

So what do you do when your family situation changes and that affects your plans? Part of the beauty of family life is precisely that it is always changing; new members arrive, people grow and mature and reach different stages in their lives—it's very fluid. You need to be flexible, in life and in business. Family life presents a lot of opportunity to reinvent yourself, and sometimes necessity really is the mother of invention. When couples move to a new area because one or the other has accepted a new job, when a child is born into a family, when one member loses a job . . . all these situations present opportunities for change, and positive change at that.

I admire people who raise children, especially those who are doing it by themselves. We have two of our own, and I've always spent a lot of time with them. Kids change your life in the most positive of ways, but they can also make you change your plans. Family is certainly another factor to take into consideration when you're thinking about your life plans. If you're about to have a baby, for example, you may not want to undertake a new venture that's going to be extremely time-consuming. Or you might—some people work best when they are overstretched. Just don't pretend that the family isn't a vital consideration.

The issue of staffing brings up a significant question: Should you work with members of your family? In our community, where family relations are so important and where so many small businesses are family owned or run, it's often an important consideration. Meanwhile, all the books on business tell you not to go into business or work with your family. And they're right. I know that probably sounds funny coming from a guy who has worked with his wife for over thirty years. I also work with my brother, and with Gloria's sister, and a lot of other relatives. In fact, my brother, Papo, and his wife, Patricia, run the finances for my business. When it works, there is nothing better. But this often doesn't work out, for a whole variety of reasons, and then you have to ask yourself: Is this business more important than my relationship with my brother, sister, wife, or whomever? Most likely, the answer is no.

Working with Gloria has been an extraordinary experience, but it hasn't always been an easy one. When I stepped off the stage to manage Gloria's career, I'd already worked with her for so long and I knew her desires, her rhythms, her tastes, her values, and her goals. Most important of all, I always, *always* had her best interests at heart, and nobody knows that better than Gloria.

But from Gloria's point of view, I know it was often tough having her husband as her manager. When you have a problem with a colleague, you can certainly confide in the person closest to you and cry on his or her shoulder. Whom was Gloria going to run to if she had a problem with her manager? But professional relationships, like marriages, are works in progress. Gloria makes the ultimate decisions about her career and her choices, and her manager has to respect that.

I once had an argument with my brother, Papo, and it lasted for years. In fact, we didn't speak to each other for five years. The rift happened after Gloria's accident and her recovery. She hadn't performed yet and we wanted to show the world that she was back, and better than ever. Gloria had overcome incredible adversity. She had almost been paralyzed for life, but through a miracle—and the skill of her doctors and her own will to get better—Gloria was not only walking; she was running and dancing again. And, of course, she was itching to perform. We were very grateful, and we were indebted to our fans for all their love and support and prayers. So we wanted to get back out on the road as a gesture of gratitude and as a celebration of life.

Papo argued that we'd lose a lot of money on such a tour. But I didn't think that making money was the most important consideration. So what it boiled down to was a difference of opinion on what really mattered at that point in our lives. That was the root of the argument. We truly didn't see eye to eye. I know Papo was looking out for our financial interests, and that was his job. But I felt he was completely missing the point as to why we wanted to go on this tour. We weren't doing it to make money. In fact, I wasn't concerned about losing money, especially so soon after my wife had nearly lost her life. We fought, and the argument ended with us not talking.

The silence between my brother and me persisted. Five years is a long time. In that period, Gloria and I had our second child, our daughter, Emily. We were stubborn and neither one of us budged. Each of us was so convinced that we were right and the other was wrong.

Finally Gloria said, "This is ridiculous. You two are brothers; you have to talk to him." And so she called him up and made us both speak to each other and resolve our differences. My brother came back to work with me, and he's the key man in our businesses. After all, he manages the checkbook. But when he came back, I said to him, "You may be my older brother, and you can even punch me out if we don't agree. But I make the final decisions for the company."

If you're going to work with family, you need to set up some ground rules and make sure you stick to them. And you need to learn how to communicate. The greatest thing human beings have is the ability to communicate and to express different points of view. But you wouldn't always know it. Ask my brother and me when we weren't talking to each other. It's ironic that in this so-called information age, we can't seem to communicate with one another. Perhaps it's not so much that we can't get our points across as it is that we don't respect one another enough to listen to someone else's point of view.

The problem when working with members of your family is that it's extremely easy for any disagreement to become personal. That's because it already is personal—you're related! When working with family, or anyone for that matter, we have to respect one another's decisions and our right to have a different opinion. I understood this, even as a child, but it is something that I really learned when I came to this country. This country guarantees us an incredible freedom to express ourselves, something that is absent in so many societies. I've known that since my childhood in Cuba, where I saw that fundamental right taken away. I am so grateful for that right—the right to express myself—that I have enormous respect for the same right of others. The only way to ensure that that right is protected is by valuing it and respecting the opinions of others, whether you like those opinions or not.

Respect is a fundamental of doing business. There has to be respect on all sides. I'm not saying it's easy; but if you don't have it, things just won't work. It's hard not to put your two cents in when someone you love has been made an offer or is trying to make a decision regarding a project. But you have to keep your opinion to yourself unless you are asked for it. Gloria makes her own decisions regarding her career. She is an intelligent woman and is sure of herself as an artist. I may recommend something, but when Gloria says no, it's her no.

I'll say it again: It's probably better not to work with family, but if you can do it effectively, there really is nothing better. After all, who could love you more than a brother? Just remember that mutual respect tops the list of ground rules that you have to make.

My niece Lili Estefan has her own show on Univision. She's very much like me, but I can't take any credit for what she's achieved. A famous last name can be a burden, that's for sure, but it can also be a blessing. Whatever you achieve, though, it is to your credit.

CHAPTER THIRTY-ONE

Reinvent Your Personal Wheel

It's only a few hours north of Miami Beach, but Vero Beach may as well be a different world. Vero Beach is a lovely old Florida town, perhaps best known for Dodgertown, where the Dodgers played spring training baseball from 1948, when they were still in Brooklyn, through 2008. Vero is on Florida's Treasure Coast, not far from Cape Canaveral and the Kennedy Space Center, and only about ninety miles from Orlando and all its attractions: amusement parks and outlet shopping. There is a small airport in Vero and several international airports within a couple of hours' drive, and the area is a major national and international tourist destination.

We found Vero a few years ago when we were looking for a getaway we could drive to easily from Miami. We found the house and completely refurbished it. One morning were driving around getting to know the town and decided to stop and have breakfast at a small, run-down hotel we spotted right on the beach, set back some from the main street. It had a driveway and small parking lot, a main lobby and restaurant and pool area, and two wings of five stories each. The Palm Court Hotel, which had been built in the seventies, was up for sale. Not that we were necessarily looking for a new project, but this one had potential written all over it. Since we were going to be spending more time up in Vero Beach, it didn't seem like a bad idea to have a stake in the community. We already owned and operated one hotel, the Cardozo, so we knew something about the hospitality business.

We purchased the Palm Court in 2004 and set about preparing to refurbish the hotel. The hotel was pretty run-down. Our plan was to make it more upscale by remodeling it and making some infrastructure improvements. The hotel has an amazing location—right on the beach—and in my mind's eye I saw something so much better than the building that was there at the time. The hotel is located along Vero's Ocean Drive, which I thought was a nice coincidence, since our other hotel, the Cardozo, is located on the world-famous street of the same name in South Beach. The one in Vero Beach has a charm all its own. Of course, when word got out that the Estefans were investing in Vero Beach, we took it on the chin again! "There goes the neighborhood! Those show-business folks are going to bring all kinds of rowdy people and their rowdy parties to the area." Well, that was not what we wanted at all. We wanted to take advantage of the calm, serene vibe there and just add our own touch.

We had an architect draw up plans to give the Palm Court a face-lift and were set to begin the overhaul in the fall of 2004. But nature had other plans. That same year, Florida was hit hard by two major hurricanes, Frances and Jeanne, which all but destroyed the Palm Court. Frances packed such a punch that the roof on one of the wings caved in. When Jeanne blew through less than two weeks later, she finished off the job, blowing out windows and demolishing the interior of most of the hotel.

The truth is I wasn't too upset about the damage the hurricanes did to the hotel. It's such a superb location for a hotel that I really believed we could make something so much more beautiful if we started almost from scratch. So I guess I got my wish.

We hired STA Architectural Group in Miami, who refurbished our house in Vero and had also done our Miami Beach offices. They understood what we liked and what we wanted to do. We went back to the drawing board. The old plans went out the window and we started almost at the beginning.

One thing Gloria and I were insistent on was making the hotel as environmentally sound as possible. We wanted to reuse and recycle materials, use local craftsmen, make it energy and water efficient, and respect the local wildlife. The house in Vero is on the beach, and we get to see turtles nest right in front of us. And it's a beautiful sight, but the turtles are very vulnerable, especially when they're nesting, so we kept that in mind when we were building and also when we were using the beach.

All the rooms that face the ocean have blackout curtains or heavy drapes, not just for the guests' comfort but for the safety of the turtles, who nest for six months of the year on the beach right in front of the hotel, laying their eggs in the sand. If they see light, they get confused, and many of them lose their way and die on the beach. So not only did we place heavy curtains in the rooms; we ask guests to lower their lights as of nine p.m. and we explain to them why.

In terms of the look and feel of the hotel, I had a very clear vision of what I wanted. The beach is white like sugar and the water is usually a light blue. The ocean in front of the hotel is often really placid, and it looks more like the Caribbean than a lot of the waters farther south. The hotel is set back from the street, which gives it an air of exclusivity, not so much like a country club but like a private club or an "in" place, something a little bit exotic but not uninviting. I knew I wanted the best of the upscale South Beach vibe, and the setting was perfect for that.

I also knew we could add something nice to the community in terms of another business, and that our business would attract other area business. The pool area would be perfect for parties, the ballroom for weddings, and a spa could be an extra business line for the hotel.

I wanted the hotel exterior to be clear and bright, not garish, just nice and simple, something that would complement the natural setting and not try to compete with it. (How could you compete with the ocean anyway?) And the hotel's interior needed to re-create a kind of tropical feel. I could imagine light colors, maybe white, cool materials like marble and wood throughout. More than anything, I wanted to design a space that I would want to be in myself. Again, I figured that if I liked it, others would too. So the design concept for the hotel is very much in tune with our own homes: clear, bright, cool, and serene.

Once we agreed on a concept with the architects, we then began talking about how we were going to carry it out. Vero Beach is part of a barrier island, a pretty thin strip of land between the Atlantic Ocean and the Indian River Lagoon, so it is an environmentally sensitive area. We didn't want to add any unnecessary stress or more waste to the area. That philosophy is an integral part of the hotel's concept and design— complementing the setting and respecting the environment.

In the design, we maintained the overall structure of the hotel: two wings of five stories each, a pool anchoring the central social area with a direct ocean view, parking at the front of the hotel, and a circular drive leading to the main entrance to the lobby and front desk. We reduced the number of rooms, making them larger than in the original hotel and creating four oceanfront suites and a presidential suite in the penthouse, with a spa and a gym added to the plans.

It was trickier than I'd thought to use local materials. I wanted a cool tropical feel, but the hotel needed to be rebuilt with strong materials, as resistant to hurricane damage as possible. We decided on marble floors (the marble was brought from Turkey) and heavy woods, like teak. But much of the rest of the materials were local, such as the finishes, some of which were created from recycled materials. (For instance, decorative finishes in some rooms are made with crushed windshield glass and are backlit; the hallways and elevators are lined with sea reeds under glass.)

We invested in Vero Beach because obviously we saw a great opportunity, but also for the same reason we invested in Miami: We had a stake in the community. When we first bought our place in Vero Beach, I don't think we really imagined that we would love it so much and that we would wind up spending so much time there. But we pretty quickly fell in love with the area and the community. And we've always felt very strongly about giving back. So when we started the actual construction on the hotel, we knew we would be creating jobs for locals, not just for the duration of the construction but hopefully long afterward as well.

One of the fun details of the construction was being able to make the furniture. I used craftsmen who had worked with us for years. I didn't want to have it made to order in China, where it would surely be cheaper. And I knew exactly what I wanted in terms of designing and building the bed platforms, the tables, and the built-in drawers. We used teak for the bed platforms, and the walls of the rooms are accented with the same wood. Some rooms and the hallways have porthole-shaped windows, which gives the hotel an overall feeling of a yacht or a cruise ship.

The building materials and all the details all helped create a very clean and uncluttered look, which I think in turn creates a very relaxed feeling, almost like a spa—nice and quiet and calm. And while the look and feel are very important, how the building functions and how we function in it are also key. Like most hotels do nowadays we placed cards in the rooms encouraging guests to reuse towels and linens, but that wasn't enough. We installed water-saving devices like low-flow toilets, and Gloria created little cards that go on the back of each toilet, explaining how to use the different flush buttons: *Press right for number two; press left for number one.*

The hotel restaurant is a mix of Cuban and Asian cuisine. The menu was created by our chef, with our input. The restaurant's name, Oriente, is the same as that of the original restaurant in our hotel in South Beach, and there are similarities in feel, but the chef created new dishes using local ingredients for Oriente in Vero Beach. We renamed the hotel Costa d'Este—*este* is "east" in Spanish (the hotel is on the East Coast), and it's also the first four letters of Estefan.

We supervised the construction of the hotel, and it was easy enough to get up to Vero Beach on a fairly regular basis to oversee progress. But for the long-term running of the business we decided we needed another plan. Hospitality is one of those organic businesses where, as an entrepreneur, you get to use a variety of talents and skill sets. I think that's a large part of the reason I enjoy it so much. This was an almost-from-scratch project, so I got to be in on it every step of the way, from negotiating the purchase of the hotel to designing and choosing building materials, working on the interiors—choosing fabrics, colors, finishing materials—the restaurant and menus, and marketing, of course.

In the past, we've had our own people—that is, people directly employed by Estefan Enterprises—running our restaurants and the hotel, the studio, real estate properties, the music business, everything. We realized we needed a full-service company to take care of running the hotel, since we could not do it remotely. Vero Beach is only about a two- or two-and-a-half-hour drive from Miami, but that's far enough that we needed someone on site, within easy reach of the business.

We met Burt Cabañas, the founder, owner, and CEO of Benchmark Hospitality International, a Houston-based management company. Burt and I clicked professionally and personally right away. Like me, he is a self-made man, an entrepreneur. He started Benchmark himself and continues to run the day-to-day operations of the company. And, like me, he is Cuban—need I say more? Burt and his company, Benchmark, provide a service for us as if we were doing it ourselves. They have the same attention to detail as does Estefan Enterprises, and they are specialists in the field. Benchmark also helps to market the property (although, of course, we are also heavily involved in that aspect of the business).

Conceiving, designing, and building a small resort is a major task. This became a $50 million project. Budgets equal time; time equals money. "Time is money" is so much more than a saying. It's a business reality. There are a whole lot of small lessons in the Vero Beach experience, but the big takeaways for me were, first, following the 2004 hurricanes, I had to plan and replan because the original concept was not going to work after the building was virtually destroyed; and, second, finishing the building didn't mean finishing the project. Once we finished the building, we still had a resort to run. Hiring a management company is not something that we have typically done for other projects (like the Cardozo or the restaurants), but the scope of the project and the distance made it not just necessary but a really sound decision.

Costa d'Este Beach Resort hotel opened on time (and on budget) in June 2008. With our hotel renovation and operation I've added another string to my business bow. To me, our hotel business has been one more business model to learn, but I haven't had to step out of my comfort zone to do it. I've taken what I learned here and used it at the Cardozo. We spent tens of millions in Vero Beach, but we're doing the Cardozo for a fraction of the cost. You can have a decorator tell you about special lights you order in from Hawaii or you can go to Home Depot and buy them yourself. When money is tight you have to spend money only when it really makes sense.

BY 2008, WHEN THE HOTEL opened, I'd been in the United States forty years. You can look back through the pages of this book and see how many times I reinvented my personal wheel. Who'd have thought when I left Cuba that I'd have gone into the hotel and hotel renovation business? This is a good place to step back and take stock of where all this has gotten me.

CHAPTER THIRTY-TWO

Take Stock and Measure Success

O n a warm evening late in the summer of 2007, Gloria and I hosted a preview screening of *90 Millas,* a documentary we had been working on for much of the previous two years that accompanied Gloria's album of the same name. The film and the album are a tribute to Cuban music, and both include the participation of Latin legends like Cachao, Arturo Sandoval, Carlos Santana, José Feliciano, Generoso Jimenez, Alfredo "Chocolate" Armenteros, Johnny Pacheco, and on and on! The screening was at the Tower Theater in Miami's Little Havana, not far from where I bought my accordion oh, so many years ago. I looked around the theater and there were a lot of friends and colleagues in attendance, old and new alike.

The documentary means a great deal to us. It is a heartfelt project about the culture and music we love. It's also our first movie, which means we've taken our music into a whole new area. We've been making videos for the last two decades, and Gloria has acted in several movies. But this was a first for us, and it was fun. A lot of fun. We spent two years traveling the country with small cameras and portable lights, documenting the recording of the album and interviewing some of those superb, impassioned musicians who bring our traditions to life. It was another real labor of love, not just for Gloria and me, but also for all who participated in the making of the movie.

Ninety miles is the distance between Key West and Cuba. As the crow flies it's not a long way, but in every other respect it's so much farther. All of us who have traveled that route have made such a long personal journey. Andy Garcia says in the film that Cuba is the impossible love, the girl you love but can't be with. Carlos Santana and José Feliciano, who play with Gloria and Sheila E. on the album's first single, "No Llores," talk in the movie about their beginnings and how hard it was to play Latin music in the United States years ago.

Puerto Rico's José Feliciano was maybe the first "crossover" star, with *Light My Fire* in 1968. José told a story about a man from the record company telling him he should change his name to Joe Philips. José said he would never dishonor his father like that. Those times are, like the ninety miles. They are similarly so far and yet so close. We share those memories, those struggles, and those successes. We have all come a very long way.

Less than a year before the movie screening, in October 2006, I produced the opening gala for the new Miami Performing Arts Center. This beautiful new venue is also walking distance from the music store where I bought the accordion. The night before the gala, as I watched stars like Bernadette Peters, Carlos Vives, Alejandro Sanz, and José Carreras rehearse, I thought of all the changes I have witnessed in Miami and, of course, how much had happened to me over the same period. Miami was at long last inaugurating a first-class concert center, one that would attract topflight local, national, and international talent. Who wouldn't want to perform in state-of-the-art concert facilities in Miami? The coincidence of producing an important event at this grand concert hall only walking distance from where I had taken the first steps of my professional career forty years earlier did not escape me. I felt a wave of gratitude. I felt satisfied. And like a kid, I felt excited.

I'm young. I still have a whole life ahead of me. And yet, I've had a very full and interesting life—so far! It feels like there is so much more to do and so much more that I want to do. I could have written those same words ten years ago, twenty years ago, and certainly thirty years ago. Today, I still feel exactly the same way.

Every time I try something new, I get a tremendous rush. If I was ever nervous about doing new things, that feeling left me a long, long time ago. But every time I produce an album or something else familiar that I really love to do, I feel I could be doing it for the first time. I get a real joy out of work.

A really fun new opportunity presented itself not long ago—the chance to venture into an entirely new area: major league sports. Steve Ross, a very successful real estate developer and now the owner and managing general partner of the Miami Dolphins, contacted us and invited Gloria and me to invest in the football team. Again, another opportunity to have a stake in the community as well as the opportunity to get involved in changing and improving a great brand.

In June 2009 we bought a minority stake in the team and we became the first Cuban-Americans to own an NFL franchise. Gloria has already jumped in with both feet! Along with Hank Williams Jr. she recorded the *Monday Night Football* theme song, "Are You Ready for Some Football." And my mind races (and my heart pounds!) just thinking of the possibilities of what one can do with a football team!

And most of all, it offers the chance for NFL to reach out to Hispanics and for Hispanics to become more familiar with this all-American sport. (I'm a longtime fan, myself!)

My birthday rolled around again this past March. I thought, "Another year older," but to me, my age is just a number. If truth be told, I'm well into my middle years, but I'm still waiting for my "midlife crisis." Somehow, I don't think I'm likely to have one. I think a midlife crisis happens only to someone who has regrets. That's not me. I have nothing to regret and only things to feel grateful for and to look forward to.

I'm still living by the principles that got me to this place. Most days I wake up and my first thought is how happy I am that I have a full day ahead. That's probably the great advantage of always planning the way I do. I have obligations to fulfill, and if you follow through, you generally feel satisfied at the day's end. Planning your life and being prepared for whatever the future brings puts you in a good place emotionally, spiritually, intellectually, financially . . . in every way. That's where I am today: looking forward to the future.

I've worked long and hard to make a name for myself, and that name and reputation are what allow me to continue to try new things. The same holds true for you. You are your own best reference, you and your track record, you and your good name. You have to learn to take that to the bank, and to strive to take yourself and your dreams to the next level and to do it continuously. There can be no stopping, and even though it is wise to plan for retirement, financially and professionally, most entrepreneurs never want to slow down. That's what makes us a breed apart. There is always another day, always another challenge, always another opportunity.

Thank God for that.

If you were to ask me what I consider my most important professional accomplishment, I would say that I believe I blazed a trail for other Latino artists into mainstream America. As doors were opened to me, I forced them open even wider for others. And what has truly motivated me professionally, as I have achieved more and more, is to see other Latino artists coming up behind me. Their success is gratifying. It is more gratifying than any monetary reward could ever be.

That kind of success, which isn't my success but the success of the larger community, is the best kind. Everyone benefits from it, from raising the level and creating awareness of all that talent. But what of your own individual success? That kind of success can be a double-edged sword. On the one hand, it will allow you to do other things. And on the other hand, you can get involved in only so much. The minute you start doing too many things too fast, you lose quality. It's more important to take time and do things right, and maybe wait out certain opportunities. Experience and judgment will be your guide.

I always talk about planning and making lists and meeting your deadlines. Those are all part of the day-to-day. But you have to see the big picture; you have to look at your life and your goals from thirty thousand feet. Having goals is so much more than checking off items on a to-do list. Meeting specific goals can be urgent, but the big picture is way more important.

We talked about it back in chapter three: How do you measure success? For some it might be the ability to sit in a bar watching a football game all afternoon or spend a lot of time on the beach. Each could be from a position of financial security or a what-the-heck attitude. These are lifestyle decisions and not what I consider to be real accomplishments. If I look at my accomplishments, I think I can feel quite satisfied with what I have done.

I have produced for TV, including events at the White House. That's a big deal for anyone—imagine what that's like for an immigrant! I've lost count of the number of events I've done with presidents. I've met and talked to President Obama. I sat and talked with President Bush (the last one) on Air Force One about the state of the country. I shared with him my concerns about the major problems in Latin America, and, of course, about Cuba. Last time I saw President Bush he asked if I was going to vote for John McCain. I said I was going to vote for Obama. Which wasn't what he wanted to hear.

I can tell you about the last five presidents from my experience. As different as each one was, I was impressed by all of them. The previous president, George W. Bush, really opened the White House to Latinos. And of course, President Obama named a Latina, Sonia Sotomayor, to the Supreme Court, a very significat and important appointment. Obama's White House has a lot of energy, a very good and positive energy, with a lot of young, smart people around. Abroad, I think Obama changed the image of the United States in about twenty-four hours. There are so many misconceptions about America and Americans, something I've never been able to understand.

What else? I've produced music for the halftime show at the Super Bowl; music for the opening and closing ceremonies of the Olympics; the Latin Grammys. I have earned nineteen Grammys and Latin Grammys myself; been named BMI Songwriter of the Year; received honorary doctorates and a star on the Hollywood Walk of Fame. The list goes on. But filling your résumé alone is not success.

Is material success the yardstick? When I first used to go to Sony for meetings when we were starting out, I would ride my bike because I didn't have enough money for gas. So being able to buy a car was certainly a step up! Buying something without having to check the price is certainly an aspect of that. That's an enjoyable by-product of success. But not having to worry about spending $300 on a pair of jeans isn't, in itself, success. And that's not to say I would necessarily just drop a couple of hundred on jeans. I won't buy things just because I can. I'm more driven by whether or not I need it, and then, do I really want it.

When I was a kid, I wanted to buy a jacket that cost what was a lot of money to us. Every day I would walk to the store with my mom to see the jacket. I said to the shop owner that I'd like to buy it on layaway, so I gave him $5 down. I saved, I scrimped—I couldn't wait to get that jacket. Finally the day came. I had the rest of the money! Of course, I hadn't counted on sales tax, which was another 4 percent. I had to wait one more week to get the rest of the money. And when I got the jacket, I realized how important every penny was to achieving that dream. When I see a penny on the street, I still bend down to pick it up. I save pennies in a jar. It reminds me that great fortunes, like big dreams, require an appreciation of small steps. It's a great feeling to be able to say, "I can get it." It's an even better feeling to say, "I don't need it."

I've seen lots of news reports estimating my net worth. To me, it isn't important; it really, truly is not important. It is more important to have goals and to complete things. Besides, money can be gone from one day to the next. As Gloria and I have discovered, life can change in an instant.

I think one great measure of success is how you react to mistakes. Everyone makes mistakes. I have made mistakes in my life, but it's usually when I didn't follow through on my instincts. When we struck the deal with Sony to start Crescent Moon Records, I agreed to the terms but with reservations because Sony controlled the purse strings, and I felt they didn't understand the Latin market well enough to make the label a success. The artists became successful, but Sony didn't promote them as much as I would have. The venture certainly wasn't a complete failure— we won many Grammys, we sold records and we helped launch the careers of artists who to this day are successful. I realize that one measure of my success is that I've earned the right to make my own mistakes.

CHAPTER THIRTY-THREE

Give Back

O ne of the best measures of success is in how you give back. So, when should you start to give back? My advice is to start to give back right away. Once you've made your first dollar, think about giving back with your second. Why? Because if you get into the habit of giving back when you don't have a lot of money, you'll get into the habit of donating your time. And it's just as important to give your time as it is to give your money. You don't want to be one of those "successful" people who at first is too broke to give money and then later too busy to give time.

We've always tried to contribute to causes that are important to us and also in moments of great need. Gloria and I have long been heavily involved in philanthropic causes, and not just as financial benefactors. We played benefit concerts as far back as our days as the Miami Latin Boys, and have continued that tradition. We have organized concerts and fund-raisers after hurricanes Andrew, George, and Katrina, as well as benefits for military families. After 9/11, I lined up about sixty artists to perform a song called "El Último Adios"—the proceeds of which went to the American Red Cross.

We continue to give back going forward. Our friend Alejandro Fernández, the international superstar, performed two concerts in Mexico in June of 2009 to show the world that it was okay to go there after the swine flu outbreak, and Gloria performed in the second show in Guadalajara.

I am actively involved in different charitable organizations as a fund-raiser as well as a benefactor. In 1993, we established the Gloria Estefan Foundation, an open-door foundation that empowers young people by offering financial support to promote good health, education, and cultural development. The foundation funds scholarships and helps abused and at-risk youth. Through the foundation, we also made a large donation to the Miami Project to Cure Paralysis, the world's most comprehensive research center dedicated to treating people with spinal cord injuries and to finding a cure for paralysis. After Gloria's accident it's obviously a cause very near and dear to us.

I'm not saying you need to set up a foundation. (Although when you get to a certain level where your revenues are sufficiently high, people call on you to get involved with the community and to contribute financially. Then it's certainly not a bad idea to set up some kind of formal mechanism to contribute.) What I really believe you need to do, from the moment you start your own business, is to be involved in the community and with the people in your path. You'll figure out what kinds of activities are closest to your heart, and also to what degree you are able to give your time and money to charitable activities. What I am telling you that you must do to be a successful person is to give back in some form and to make giving a goal alongside growing your business. Giving back is part and parcel of success.

SO MANY PEOPLE COME UP to me spontaneously and say thanks for all we've done for "our people"—not just Cubans but all Latinos. A young woman tapped on the window of my car one day, I think she was Colombian, and she said, "God bless you, and thanks." An older Cuban man in a tollbooth on the causeway in Miami gave me his hand and said, "May God give you back all that you have done for others." Once, as I was going into an event at the Kennedy Center in Washington, several waiters started to make a fuss over me. "Emilio, Emilio," they called out. All those things fill me up; they are worth more than you can imagine. And it only makes me want to do more.

But it isn't being recognized that is gratifying. It is the realization that I have accomplished something important that makes me feel fulfilled. Fame is irrelevant. Not long ago a woman recognized me and came over to say hello. She was very excited and said to her little girl, "Go ahead—ask for an autograph." The little girl looked up at me and said, "Who are you?" That put things in perspective!

Fame is a gift, as long as you use it in the right way and don't take it too seriously. Some careers make people very famous and highly visible. But that doesn't mean they will leave any lasting legacy. And there are careers that have very low visibility, but they can still leave an incredible imprint on the world. The best legacy you can leave is to do as much good as you can.

My people are also my family. My Latino community. I feel so close and so united to my community, and it's not just my fellow Cuban-Americans I feel close to, but all Latinos. Whenever I see artists win a Grammy or another award and they say, "I dedicate this to my country, Colombia," or Mexico or whatever country they are from. I can't do that. How can I dedicate a win to Cuba? Cuba is my country, where I was born, so much of what formed me. But no. It is still run by a repressive regime, and it is such a frustration and source of sadness not to be able to thank the land of my birth and credit it for my accomplishments. But I have my people, my community, my country, in the Latinos here. So many Colombians, Puerto Ricans, Dominicans, and others have been such an important part of my growth and my success. And they have embraced me and honored me and adopted me in their home countries. I arrive in those places and feel at home. The respect and affection and recognition are more than I could have hoped for. What more could I possibly ask for?

I realized one of my biggest dreams fairly early on, and that gave me a lot of peace. Getting my family out of Cuba and making enough money for all of us to get on our feet were the original motivations that caused me to drive myself so hard to get ahead. My mother was finally able to leave years after my father and I settled in Miami. She left Cuba for Mexico and crossed the border between the United States and Mexico by foot with a coyote. No one could have been more supportive of my dreams and my ambitions than my mother. She had extraordinary patience and optimism. It never wavered; she never doubted that everything would turn out right.

Few things gave me more pleasure than picking up my parents in the evenings and taking them out for ice cream. We enjoyed one another's company so much; driving to get ice cream with them, all of us together, that often felt like a dream come true. Yes, it truly was that simple for me. That was success for me. To this day, those memories, so sweet, are among the greatest measures of my success. The man had accomplished what the child had set out to do.

I have achieved the most important dream of all—having my family together, and together in a free country. Both my parents are gone now. Losing my dad left a terrible scar, even though he lived a long and good life—I still miss him to this day. And my mother died much more recently. That still hurts too, of course. But they were able to share in my American dream, something for which I am deeply grateful. Still, my ambitions and motivations remain the same. I am driven to succeed for my family, and now also for all my employees and their families and, of course, our fans. My son, Nayib, is now all grown-up but one is always a father, just as I was always a son to my parents. I am proud of Nayib and how hard he works and the life he has built for himself. Emily is still young—so I guess that means I am too. When you are raising a teenager, you realize how truly young at heart you can be. She still has time at home with us, but that too will fly by. Gloria knows what balance is: She has had success with several beautiful children's books and is writing film scripts. She is truly a gifted writer. And she also dedicates herself to what she says she loves best—being a mom. Her priority is taking care of our miracle baby, Emily.

I grew my personal life alongside my professional life. That was a conscious decision. It didn't just happen. And all that I have today, personally and professionally, didn't happen overnight. Loving what I do, being true to myself and my culture, thinking big and working hard got me where I am today. And all those things will keep me there and take me to the next level too.

CHAPTER THIRTY-FOUR

Look to the Future

T he entertainment industry in general, and the music industry in particular, have both suffered major losses in recent years because of the way people are accessing content. The only way to recoup those losses and promote new artists is to use new technology like the Internet and cell phones to our advantage. The music industry for too long ignored file sharing and other technological advances, to its peril.

One of the most exciting and challenging aspects of the entertainment industry is that consumers are demanding, and not just in what they want to spend their time watching, listening to, and reading. They are demanding about how to enjoy entertainment. That's a good thing. And we in the entertainment business need not only to keep surprising consumers with great content; we have to figure out how to make it available to them in the easiest, most affordable ways possible.

Right now, consumers are kind of drunk on technology. There is so much out there and it's so easy to access, and traditional media is suffering as a result. New media threatens the existence of old media. Look at what has happened to TV networks. And newspapers have been closing at an alarming rate all over the country.

Once traditional media fully embraces new media the industry will probably find its way. Anybody can create a blog now. But can they drive traffic to their site on an ongoing basis? The same is happening in entertainment. The new generation needs to take advantage of this. Any kid with a guitar and a voice can make a video, post it, and, if it's good (or really, really bad) it will go viral. The entertainment industry will figure technology out, and consumers will buy the best content out there. Where all media lags behind right now is in its use of technology. I hope that record companies in particular will get their act together, because the way things are going now, in a few years they won't exist.

Businesses often make the dangerous assumption that people are going to keep on buying their products, so they get complacent about consumers and take them for granted. As great a product as you have, and as successful as it is, you have to always keep your eye on the future. That means that you not only have to spot trends and embrace them; you have to help create them.

I don't spend a lot of time looking back. I'm always too excited about the future. But when I do look back to when I first started in the music business, I feel almost overwhelmed by how far we've all come. A lot of that has to do with the exciting new multimedia world we live in; a lot has to do with globalization and people moving around the world and becoming exposed to other cultures and tastes. Whatever the reasons, there is now a lot more appreciation for a much more diverse offering of music, movies, fashion, and food than there ever was before. That's the world we're living in now. It's an exciting time to be alive and to be creating.

As an entrepreneur, you can't just focus on growing your company. You also have to expend energy on helping to grow the market. You need to help grow the market in order to gain consumers, but also because you believe in what you are doing, and it is natural that you want more people to get it too. The bigger the market for your idea, the more money will be invested in improving and marketing what you are doing.

When we first started recording albums, the budget for a comparable English-language album was probably $200,000, and for Latin music it was about $20,000 (and remember, a lot of us pioneers had to front a huge chunk of that money!). We've come a long way, baby, but it sure wasn't easy. New ideas meet with resistance, and success meets with envy. Both of those are inevitable, and you're going to have to learn to deal with them. Successful people are often looked upon with envy and are often victims of nasty remarks. "Oh, he was lucky," some might say. Or, "He had connections." As hurtful as such comments might be, don't let them discourage you. But when you take the lead, as I have on many things, you can't escape controversy, so prepare yourself.

HERE IS A PRACTICAL QUESTION: Where is there a need for new ideas? I would say that just about every industry and sector is ripe for innovation. Services, technology, and marketing are all areas of tremendous growth and competition. And keep in mind that there is always room for good ideas, no matter how crowded a field might seem.

The world is changing faster than ever these days. It sure isn't what it was when I started working almost four decades ago. We are closer to one another than ever before, and there is an unstoppable trend to make it easier and easier for people to connect with one another, as much for business as for personal reasons.

The service industry (hospitality, tourism, banking, retail, to name a few branches) is experiencing a real boom, in large part because of globalization. So much of what is now called outsourcing is actually a new way to carry out a service.

There are so many great ideas out there that weren't around as recently as ten or fifteen years ago: businesses plans, ways to do business, even where people are doing business. More and more people are working for themselves, and they are doing it remotely (that is, not in your office, maybe not even in your zip code or even your time zone). They usually have more than one "boss"—they develop a roster of clients or customers. Many accountants, for instance, work out of their own offices and have multiple clients. Most small to medium-size businesses, those that make up the backbone of our economy and our country, can't afford to keep an accountant in full-time employ. So accounting—a service—has become very innovative in recent years. There are now many accounting offices that are paperless, which appeals to me as an environmentalist. (And for some years now, you've been able to file your income taxes electronically!)

Did you know that you can get an executive assistant or concierge to organize your agenda for you remotely? All it takes is a phone call or an e-mail. There is so much innovation going on in the service industry. (I think, however, that it's going to be a while before we outsource waiters. Not a particularly good or practical idea, is it?) You don't necessarily need to invent a new position, but having someone work for you on a part-time basis from a remote location is a new way to carry out that function.

The area that has allowed much of the innovation in the service industry, as well as so many other industries, is, of course, technology. Advances in technology, particularly in the last two decades, have made our lives less cluttered and less complicated in so many ways. (You have to make technology your slave, not the other way around.) The greater availability of computers and the Internet, increased competition in phone services, online banking, paying your taxes online, ordering your groceries online—those are just a few great ideas and innovations that have made modern life easier.

Those of us in entertainment have benefited so much from technological advances. Technology has not only reinvented the way we make and record music; it has revolutionized how we listen to music (MP3 players, for example) and, maybe even more important, how we buy music (downloads, for example—when was the last time you were in a "record store"?). And ring tones? Now, there's a big business!

All those changes and innovations are fantastic, and I couldn't be more excited about the way technology and services are improving our lives.

There is a lot to be said for simplicity too. Whoever came up with the idea of a flat rate for services, like gyms, hit on a great thing. People can use a service as much or as little as they like, so it benefits them as much as they allow it to. And the service benefits because it can count on those revenues and it doesn't lose if the client uses the service a lot or a little.

Some technologies have, fortunately, come and gone (eight-track, anyone?), but others remain and will even be recycled. I find myself thinking a lot these days about how we blend the old and the new. Remember shopping by mail? You would receive a catalog, order by mail, and your item would be delivered by mail. Well, look at online shopping. With few exceptions, when you shop online you are still going to need postal or messenger services for delivery. There is a blend of the old (mail) with the new (Internet).

There are so many good ideas out there, right within your reach. The saying, "There's nothing new under the sun" is only half-true. There are plenty of new ways of doing things, new uses for old things, and ways to blend the old with the new. Don't forget the mantra: Recycle, renew, revive. I think about how we recorded *90 Millas*. I recorded the sound on the best modern equipment the recording industry has to offer and then transferred the mix to old two-inch tapes. We had the quality of the new equipment and the warmth of the old. Old and new together creating magic.

Of course, any talk about the future has to take account of something we have no real way of predicting: the current global recession. We are going through tough economic times, and there is an awful lot of uncertainty about what the future holds. I am convinced that times of crisis can offer great opportunity for those who are creative, thoughtful, resourceful, and organized. Now is the moment for you to create. This is the time to be fearless, to carry out your dream. Credit is tight and investors are nervous, but people are also weary of the negativity out there. You might be surprised at how receptive the market could be to a new idea right now. What are you waiting for? There is no time like the present.

Tough times challenge you to be more creative. So don't be afraid—get motivated! Be inspired! Because we also live in great times. There is so much room for innovation and counterintuitive thinking right now. I looked at the takings at our restaurant Larios and I saw they were down. The recession was biting. Conventional wisdom would have been to cut spending and costs and consolidate. Out of the box, I thought, "Let's remodel!" We spruced it up—more umbrellas, more fans, more fun. People told me I was crazy, but when we opened with the new look, we broke our one-day-takings record.

If your business principles were good to begin with then you'll be in better shape. If banks had been more frugal and not encouraged people into crazy levels of borrowing, then we could have been in better shape. And if the people borrowing money had thought twice, the same would be true. Take our real estate investments. When I bought, I bought location. I bought on Ocean Drive, and the location's still good. So remember all those positives and don't lose your enthusiasm.

Conclusion

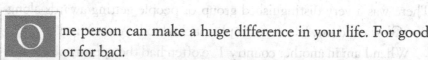ne person can make a huge difference in your life. For good or for bad.

If I can inspire one person with this book, then the time and effort I have put into it will be worthwhile. I talk to people all the time: in planes, walking on the street, going into a building for a meeting. When I'm in Miami I ride my bike or walk to the beach every day, and I talk with the homeless guys I meet there. I meet kids who are the age I was when I left Cuba for Spain, and when I talk to them I hope I can instill some of the lessons I've learned over the years. If someone gets inspired by something I have to say, I'm happy.

There are a few messages I want to get across in my book. But none of them is more important to me than my expression of gratitude to the United States. I want to tell my story and tell people how I found success. I want the story of my life to inspire people. But I also want to say thank you to the United States for taking me in and giving me all the opportunities I've enjoyed over the last forty-plus years.

I arrived here as an immigrant with nothing but the willingness to work and the drive to succeed, and America provided me with the opportunities.

I could stop working right now and I would have done more than I could possibly have imagined back when I left Cuba. When I first got to

Miami and saw all the opportunity and heard stories of other people who came with only the clothes on their backs—as I did—and had enormous successes, I couldn't have imagined all the wonderful things that have happened to me.

In May of 2009, Gloria and I were honored by the Statue of Liberty–Ellis Island Foundation for what they called "contributions to the American tapestry." The occasion was the eight annual Ellis Island Family Heritage Awards, which are given to immigrants who came to the United States through Ellis Island and their descendants. Gloria and I were honored to get a special presentation called the B. C. Forbes Peopling of America Award, which is given to someone who immigrated to this country around the Ellis Island period (in our case a few years later). There was a very distinguished group of people getting awards alongside Gloria and me. We were deeply touched to be recognized.

When I am in another country, I've often had the opportunity to talk about this country, and more often than not it is to clear up misconceptions. People in the United States are surprisingly humble in so many ways, and by and large they are very, very grateful for their opportunities. I always let people know, here and abroad, that we live in the best country in the world. I'm happy to say that. That doesn't mean that the country and its people are perfect, but I have so much pride in everything this country represents.

I marvel at this country. It truly is the land of opportunity like no other. Believe me, there are few places in the world that I haven't been to. Is there any other country in the world that has been so generous to so many people? I am grateful that this country let me in. I am grateful for what it has given me and what it has taught me. I have learned so much about structure, but I have also been able to maintain my own ways and traditions. I am grateful for my American structure and for my Latin heart. I am grateful that my rights have been recognized and protected. And do you know how I pay back this wonderful country? By believing in the American dream.

We immigrants have so much faith in the United States; I sometimes think we have more faith in this country and its promise than many people who were born here. I do believe that I could have been successful anywhere, but not to the same extent as in the United States. This country values entrepreneurship and it rewards risk takers and those who create opportunities for themselves and others.

So many people have come to this country looking for a better way of life. Others, like me, have come here looking for freedom. The new generation coming to this country—especially the Latinos coming here—have so much to offer and so much to be proud of. We have to hold our heads high and teach people who we are and what we can do. I feel so much pride when I see the achievements of Latinos in this country: holding positions of power in government, working as doctors, lawyers, architects, engineers, becoming stars in the sports and entertainment industries, and now there is a Latina on the highest court in the land. We should feel no shame for who we are, none whatsoever.

I believe it's easier now than it used to be for Latinos in this country. One in five people in this country will be Latino by 2030, and as a result we are getting greater influence and power in government and politics and civic life.

When I arrived in this country, there was no Hispanic market as such. There were only a handful of radio stations, and in Miami there was only one Spanish-language radio station on AM. But the panorama is different these days. The Hispanic market is huge. There are Spanish-speaking television and radio stations catering to the ever-growing Hispanic market. Corporations of any size have to gear part of their sales efforts to Latinos if they're not going to lose out on a lot of business. Companies run ads and create Web sites in Spanish; they provide for Hispanic tastes in food and music; they respect the traditions of peoples from all Latin American countries.

I am so proud of all the opportunities we have been given, but I am even prouder of the opportunities we have created for ourselves and for others. There are many familiar Latino names in entertainment, fashion, and sports. But Latinos have also made enormous contributions in all fields. Nowadays there are Latinos in important positions in corporate

America, heading up Fortune 500 companies and also running their own small businesses.

In forty years in this country I've never taken anything for granted. Freedom is the main thing in life, and freedom is what defines this country. Getting to the United States was a long-held goal for me and my family. We strived hard to get here and I changed continents twice— from Cuba to Spain and from Spain to America—to make it a reality. My immigrant story is part of what was arguably the only mass middle-class migration this country has ever experienced. Lawyers, doctors, businessmen, and so many others left Cuba in a very short period. Those people felt and feel gratitude for the opportunities they were given, and they were willing to do whatever they had to to make sure their children prospered in this country. Even if it meant doing jobs like sweeping floors or pumping gas—not jobs professionals typically did! But they were willing to do it.

The Cuban immigrant community has been the most aggressive of any group, because everything was taken from us. I left Cuba with one T-shirt and one pair of pants. Cuba took everything from us—money, life, freedom. I've visited the White House many times over the years. When I was there last I said to President Obama that he should listen to three generations of Cubans to get a good perspective on the situation. There are people of my parents' generation who knew what life was like before Castro, then people of my and Gloria's generation who left when they were young, and then our children, who were born in this country. Those of our parents' generation were the ones who made the greatest sacrifices. Those of my generation, well, we were able to continue our education in our new country. But all three generations love Cuba, even if they don't know it, as my children don't, for they have never been there. We all want what is best for Cuba, and that is freedom: the freedom to speak freely, the freedom to do business, and most of all the freedom to choose their own government.

Cuban immigrants who were denied freedom are much less likely to take the freedom we have in this country for granted. It's like getting sick. Until you get sick you take your healthy life for granted. You wake up, you have a cup of coffee, everything's fine. Then you get sick and you don't even take that morning cup of coffee for granted anymore. Living in freedom is the same for most people—they don't really appreciate it until it's gone. I don't take anything for granted, certainly not my freedom. Since Gloria's terrible accident in 1990, when I wake up every morning, I thank God I'm alive.

I believe this was a very innocent country until September 11. It didn't matter where we were born or where we came from, on September 11 you saw everyone come together. On that day the innocence of the country was lost and we were less likely to take what we have for granted.

The United States and its people are incredibly welcoming, contrary to what many in the rest of the world might think. This country has been so generous to newcomers. While we need immigration reform urgently, it has to be done in a peaceful and organized way so that the country, its people and immigrants all benefit.

It is a privilege to live in a country where you weren't born, that's not your own by birth. We immigrants should be humble. So many of us, in coming to the United States, have gained opportunities and freedom that we would not have enjoyed in our own lands. We must be grateful for this; it is truly humbling to be welcomed in this way.

I remember my mom said to me before I came to this country, "Please don't get into any trouble. The country is being good enough to take you in; you should be humble in return." So I respected the country and gave back to it. I did exactly what she said. I wish my mom had been alive to see me get the award at Ellis Island.

When I arrived in this country there was no window for Latin music. We were very persistent; we believed in what we were doing. Most people said no to us, and it's when they said no that I did it and became very successful. I love a challenge. I love to reinvent and prove myself over and over using the positive energy that drives everything I do. I believe when you wake up in the morning and say, "This is going to happen," then it happens. That's the way I am.

A few times in my life, the negative could have taken over. In March of 1990, Gloria and I were on the front page of the *Miami Herald* two days in a row. The first time was a picture of my family with President George H. W. Bush in the Oval Office. The next day was a picture of our coach after it had been destroyed by a tractor-trailer and Gloria was critically injured in the hospital. I know never to take anything for granted.

I think back to the time I left Havana with my dad, and I looked out of the window of the airplane at my homeland retreating beneath the wheels of the plane as it took off and I never thought I'd see my mother again. I replaced the terrible sadness I felt that day with music and created the rhythm of my own success. My only regret is the years my mother wasted living in Cuba before she could come and share my dream in freedom. I remember her the same way I would like to be remembered myself, with a smile.

While this is the best country in the world, Cuba remains so close to my heart. I look to the sky, the same way I did as a kid. In the same way that I was looking for my own freedom, I now look for freedom in the land of my birth. In my musical career I've worked to pay tribute to my heritage. Music represents to me the place I was born, the experiences I had with my parents, and the sounds that I heard growing up. I respect that so much; it is who I am.

I've always had a love for life, enthusiasm, vision, and the desire to create something different, even when I was a boy in Santiago de Cuba and didn't know too much about the world beyond my own. No dream was ever too unobtainable or absurd. If I wanted to do something, I began by believing I could. I arrived in the United States with the clothes on my back and nothing but a suitcase full of dreams and a heart filled with hope and optimism. That, it seems, was enough.

I am so grateful to everyone who has helped me to realize my dreams, especially to my family who have always motivated, inspired and sustained me.

I was blessed to be born in Cuba. But I am so grateful to the country that I have adopted and embraced, and which has adopted and embraced me right back. God bless America.

Photo by Gio Alma

Emilio Estefan is a nineteen-time GRAMMY Award–winning producer, CEO and founder of Estefan Enterprises. He owns several companies across a broad spectrum of industries, including music publishing, restaurants, hotels, hospitality management, and real estate. For thirty years, he has shared his life with his wife, Gloria Estefan.